Murder Deferred

A Play

by
STUART READY

SAMUEL FRENCH

LONDON
NEW YORK   TORONTO   SYDNEY   HOLLYWOOD

Copyright © 1976 by Samuel French Ltd
All Rights Reserved

MURDER DEFERRED is fully protected under the copyright laws of the British Commonwealth, including Canada, the United States of America, and all other countries of the Copyright Union. All rights, including professional and amateur stage productions, recitation, lecturing, public reading, motion picture, radio broadcasting, television and the rights of translation into foreign languages are strictly reserved.

ISBN 978-0-573-03020-8

www.samuelfrench.co.uk

www.samuelfrench.com

FOR AMATEUR PRODUCTION ENQUIRIES

UNITED KINGDOM AND WORLD
EXCLUDING NORTH AMERICA

plays@SamuelFrench-London.co.uk

020 7255 4302/01

Each title is subject to availability from Samuel French, depending upon country of performance.

CAUTION: Professional and amateur producers are hereby warned that MURDER DEFERRED is subject to a licensing fee. Publication of this play does not imply availability for performance. Both amateurs and professionals considering a production are strongly advised to apply to the appropriate agent before starting rehearsals, advertising, or booking a theatre. A licensing fee must be paid whether the title is presented for charity or gain and whether or not admission is charged.

The professional rights in this play are controlled by Samuel French Ltd, 52 Fitzroy Street, London, W1T 5JR.

No one shall make any changes in this title for the purpose of production. No part of this book may be reproduced, stored in a retrieval system, or transmitted in any form, by any means, now known or yet to be invented, including mechanical, electronic, photocopying, recording, videotaping, or otherwise, without the prior written permission of the publisher. No one shall upload this title, or part of this title, to any social media websites.

The right of Stuart Ready be identified as author of this work has been asserted in accordance with Section 77 of the Copyright, Designs and Patents Act 1988.

CHARACTERS

Leila Markham, licensee of "The Hay Wain"
Mrs Bolders
Beryl Fountain
Minnie Akers
Ruth Cousins
Bridget Clancy
Trudi Bauer, a Swiss student

Note: If desired, the parts of Beryl Fountain and Bridget Clancy can be played as men, named Colonel Fountain and Mick Clancy respectively, the few necessary adjustments being made in the text.

The action takes place in Leila Markham's sitting room in "The Hay Wain", an inn in a Dorset village

ACT I
Scene 1   Friday evening
Scene 2   Saturday morning

ACT II   Saturday evening

ACT III   Sunday morning

Time – the present

ACT I

Scene 1

Leila Markham's sitting-room in "The Hay Wain", an inn in a Dorset village. Friday evening, autumn

There is a long, low window RC of the back wall. Through this one can see garden shrubs. Downstage in the R wall is a door leading to the bar area. Above the door is a cabinet containing drinks, bottles, etc. Well up in the L wall a door leads to the private quarters. Between this door and the window there is a comfortable chintz-covered settee. Above the cabinet R is a small cupboard. In the middle of the room there is a low table with an armchair R of it. Just below the L door there is a desk, with a chair facing it. Below the desk is another armchair. The room is bright and comfortable and there is a suggestion of 'period' in its fittings. Some light can still be seen through the uncurtained window

During business hours some noise from the bar area can be heard every time the door leading to it is opened

When the Curtain rises the room is empty. The telephone bell rings. Leila Markham enters R and goes to the phone on the desk. She is the licensee of "The Hay Wain"; a pleasant, good-looking woman in her middle or late thirties

Leila (*on the phone*) Hay Wain.... Yes, this is Leila Markham speaking. ... Oh, I see. Well, I'm very sorry, but I can't put people up. This is only a small inn and I haven't the accommodation.... Look, I don't want to be unhelpful, but it's quite out of the question.... (*The caller rings off and she replaces the receiver*)

Amy Bolders comes in from the bar. She is a local woman who does odd jobs at the inn. She might be any age between forty-five and fifty-five

What do they think this is? The Hilton?
Mrs Bolders Clancy wants a bottle of liqueur brandy.
Leila (*staring*) A what?
Mrs Bolders Brandy—liqueur, she said. There's none in the storeroom, she says.
Leila I should think not. This is Helford Abbas, not Piccadilly. Sure you've got it right, Mrs Bolders?
Mrs Bolders What she said, m'dear.
Leila Oh, well; if someone wants to wash down their hamburger with a liqueur brandy, who am I to stop them? (*She goes to the cupboard*)

Mrs Bolders Maybe Clancy fancies a drop herself.
Leila Clancy's poison is whisky—Irish, if she can get it. (*Bringing a bottle*) How are things in the bar?
Mrs Bolders 'Bout usual Friday evening. The odd motorist drops in. It's somethin' to watch Clancy workin' it so's they buys her a drink.
Leila (*giving her the bottle*) Now, now, Mrs Bolders. Bridget Clancy may be a bit too Irish, but she does her job behind a bar counter.
Mrs Bolders (*doubtfully*) H'm.
Leila If it were not for her being there, I should have to spend all my time pulling beer-handles.
Mrs Bolders That ain't all, m'dear.
Leila Come on, forget it. We all have people we don't much like, but don't have it in for Clancy.
Mrs Bolders That young Frenchie o' yourn . . .
Leila (*patiently*) Swiss, Mrs Bolders. Get it into your thick skull that Trudi is not a French name.
Mrs Bolders Name don't make no difference. Young girl, ain't she? An' she ain't no business to make a friend o' the likes o' Clancy. I seen 'em out together, in the village an' on walks . . .
Leila If my staff are friendly towards each other, it suits me.
Mrs Bolders Eighteen, that young girl, an' as for Clancy . . . She bin mixed up in some queer things in 'er time, you bet your life . . .
Leila (*pointedly*) Mrs Bolders, there's someone out in that bar dying for a liqueur brandy.
Mrs Bolders I only talks about what I sees, Mrs Markham, an' some things ain't for good.
Leila All right. Now be a dear, good woman and take that bottle where it's wanted.

Mrs Bolders goes off to the bar. While Leila's back is turned, the figure of Ruth Cousins appears at the window. She is twenty-five or under, hard and cunning. Her speech is uneducated, and her "trendy" appearance hardly conceals a tough and potentially dangerous young criminal

Leila turns, and sees Ruth

Ruth moves out of sight

Leila goes to the window, opens it, and looks out. There is a knock at the door R

(*Closing the windows*) Come in.

Minnie Akers and Beryl Fountain come in. Minnie Akers is a local antique dealer. She can be anything between forty and sixty. She is careless in her dress, and her sharp tongue hides a genuinely warm-hearted person. Beryl Fountain also can be any age between forty and sixty. She is a J.P. and

Act I, Scene 1 3

a woman of some importance in a small community. A woman of "class", with a slightly austere exterior

Fountain Disturbing your precious leisure?
Leila No, no; do come in.

Mrs Fountain drops easily into the armchair by the table. Mrs Akers wanders over to the desk, picks up a little figurine and examines it

Leila Money, Mrs Fountain?
Fountain Hey, who said anything about money?
Leila No-one, but I can sense you clutching a receipt book.
Fountain You're a sharp one. Well, you did say you wanted to join the Dorset Society.
Leila Of course. And I've got the cheque all made out. (*She goes to the desk and takes out a cheque*) Maybe I can sell that to Miss Akers and still show a profit?
Akers This? Don't make me laugh. Where did you get it—Bognor Pier?
Fountain Do you have to be so damned rude, Akers?
Akers She knows me. Oh, she'll give us a drink whatever I say about her knick-knacks.

Leila goes to Fountain with the cheque

Fountain Can't take you anywhere. (*As Leila comes over with the cheque*) Thanks, my dear; I'll drop a receipt in later. Glad to have you as a member. You're the sort of person we want in the Society. You agree, Akers?
Akers What? (*She is casting a professional eye over pictures and porcelain on the back wall*) Oh, sure, sure. But wait and see first if she gets the gin out.
Leila On the way, Miss Akers. (*She goes to the cabinet and takes out a bottle and glasses. Then she stops short and goes to look out of the window*)
Fountain Expecting someone?
Leila No. (*She goes to the table*) No, it's all right. Only I caught sight of some woman peering in at the window.
Fountain Oh, trippers. They regard any old pub as being of historical interest. I don't suppose they were out to rob you.
Akers (*with a sniff*) Wouldn't find much here.
Fountain Look, Akers, you may be an antique dealer but it doesn't prevent you having manners.
Akers Sorry, sorry. My manners'll take a turn for the better if I spot something worth having.
Leila How about a gin and tonic—free?
Akers It's a deal.

Leila pours out drinks and hands them out

Fountain How long have you been in Helford Abbas, Mrs Markham?
Leila Oh—three years.
Fountain Where were you before that?
Leila Here and there. A wanderer, you might say. But I came here from London.
Akers (*lifting her glass*) Cheers.
Fountain Well, you've settled down very well. Fitted in. I mean, it's always a gamble what sort of person we get taking *The Hay Wain*. We've had all sorts, haven't we, Akers?
Akers We have. Mostly alcoholics. (*Simulating a shaking hand*) Look what it's reduced me to. Either that or they kept their private gin bottle under armed guard.
Leila (*after a pause*) Did you stop in the bar as you came in?
Fountain For a moment. I had a word with old Sewell about his lumbago. We didn't have a drink, if that's what you mean.
Akers We didn't. What! With our sights set on a free one in here?
Leila No, I didn't mean that, only...
Akers Only what?
Leila Well, we had rather a strange order—liqueur brandy. I wondered if you...
Akers Liqueur brandy? Wasn't me.
Fountain Wait a minute. There was a young woman asking about brandy. I shouldn't have thought anything of it if you hadn't mentioned it.
Leila Oh, it's probably nothing. (*After a pause*) A young woman? With one of those peaked, trendy caps?
Akers Oh, God knows.
Fountain Yes, that's right. She was talking to your Bridget Clancy. Why? What's odd, except for asking for stuff like that at a village pub?
Leila (*obviously a little uneasy*) Nothing. Just that—just that I think the woman who looked through my window had a peaked cap.
Fountain (*with a shrug*) I'm a J.P., but I wouldn't suggest arresting a woman for looking through a window—or for wearing a peaked cap.
Akers I'd shoot 'em on sight. Bloody awful-looking things.
Fountain What with? You don't own anything more lethal than your own tongue.
Akers Want a bet?
Fountain (*rising*) Oh, come on, Akers, we've held up Mrs Markham long enough.
Akers No, no; you challenged me. (*She fumbles in her carrier-bag and produces a period pistol*) Reach, the pair of you.
Fountain (*impressed*) Oh! Now look at that.
Akers Seventeen-sixteen. Genuine period piece, and in full working order.
Fountain Oh, I want that. I really want that. Let me have a look at it.
Akers (*pulling it back*) In my shop, dear, and over your open cheque book.
Fountain How much?
Akers H'm—three figures.
Fountain You're a shark. I ought to have you put away.

Akers (*turning to Leila*) How about you? If you've got prowlers looking in your window, this is a damned sight better than a plastic paperweight.
Leila Just a period piece, Miss Akers. You'd be better off with a bow and arrow.
Akers (*putting on an act*) All right, all right. So you wants de hot play, man? Jes' back up nice an' steady.

Akers advances towards Leila, who laughingly backs towards the desk

How come you think this is not better for guarding your china dogs and your present from Brighton? Go on, reach, I said!

Pinned back against the desk, Leila puts her right hand behind her and pulls open a drawer

Leila Sure, I'll reach, old timer. How's this? (*When she reveals her right hand she has a pistol in it*)
Akers (*taken aback*) Oh, my Gawd!
Leila (*laughing*) Got you there, Miss Akers.
Fountain (*coming forward*) I say, is that real?
Leila Real enough. It belonged to my father. In the war.
Fountain Well, well. That's put your nose out of joint, Akers. May I see it?
Leila Sure. But be careful; it's loaded.
Fountain Loaded?
Leila I do keep it for protection, you know.

Mrs Fountain lays the pistol in the palm of her hand and looks at it

Fountain You're not joking?
Leila No; it's been loaded for years. Only hope I never have to use it.
Fountain (*seriously*) Got a licence?
Leila Well—no, I suppose I haven't.
Fountain Hey, hey. Look, my dear, I don't want to come the heavy, but I am a J.P. Not the best person in the world to show this to, am I?
Leila (*with a grimace*) No.
Fountain Well, take my advice and lock it away safely. Nasty things have been known to happen with loaded pistols that are not under proper care.
Leila (*nodding*) I know what you mean.
Akers Oh, damn it, she's not going to take pot-shots at drunks in the bar.
Fountain (*a little sharply*) I'm not joking.

The door to the bar opens and Ruth Cousins stands there

Leila has the pistol in her hand, and since it is for her to speak first there is quite a long silence

Leila This is a private room.
Cousins The woman at the bar told me to go straight in.

Leila (*her anger rising*) Did she!
Cousins You can put that gun away; I'm not a bank robber.

The seemingly innocent remark affects Leila. She puts the pistol in the drawer and closes it forcibly

Leila What do you want?
Cousins (*coolly*) See you, that's all.
Fountain (*hastily*) Well, come along, Miss Akers; we've held up Mrs Markham quite long enough.
Leila There's absolutely no reason why you should go.
Fountain Nonsense, my dear. You've got things to do and so have we. (*Going to the bar door*) We'll be seeing you.
Akers (*draining the last of her drink*) Sure, we'll be seeing you.

Akers and Fountain exit R

Cousins Why the gun-play?
Leila I don't think that's any concern of yours. And I regard it as an impertinence for you to barge in here.
Cousins Like I said, the Mick at the bar said it would be all right.
Leila Well, it's not! This is a private room.
Cousins (*glancing round the room*) Ah-ha.
Leila (*sharply*) Now, come on. What do you want?
Cousins Just a room for the night.
Leila Out of the question. I don't let rooms. You could have got that information at the bar.
Cousins (*jerking her head towards the bar door*) She said you might make an exception.
Leila She had no right . . .! (*She turns away and busies herself tidying the desk*)
Cousins Not exactly the friendly welcome at an inn, is it? Correct me if I'm wrong, but I thought anyone had the right to enquire at a reasonable-looking pub.
Leila (*turning*) It was you who was looking in at that window, wasn't it?
Cousins Didn't know I was exactly looking-in. I thought it looked quite a picturesque old place, so I gave it the once-over. People do that most anywhere without getting shot at.
Leila This is quite absurd . . . You phoned earlier, didn't you?

Cousins nods

Then why didn't you take no for an answer then?
Cousins 'Cos I never take no for an answer if it's not the answer I want.
Leila That sounds to me distinctly like a threat.
Cousins (*with a laugh*) Oh, come on. Just a shakedown for the night, a bit of breakfast, and off.
Leila (*rather too forcibly for the situation*) I have no spare room.

Act I, Scene 1

Cousins The Mick said you had. Two bedrooms and a bathroom up there.
Leila The other bedroom is my daughter's...
Cousins Who's away at boarding-school. I can pay for the change of sheets.
Leila (*going quickly to the bar door and opening it*) There's another inn at the end of the village. I suggest you enquire there.
Cousins Last word?
Leila There's nothing more to be said.
Cousins Pity. I'd taken a fancy to the place. (*Going slowly over to the door*) Student—you know. Doing a thesis on interesting village inns. And I haven't come across anything more interesting than this.
Leila Good morning.
Cousins Sure. Perhaps we'll meet sometime.

Cousins goes out

Leila closes the door sharply. She is visibly disturbed. She pours out a drink, then she puts the glass down and opens the bar door again

Leila (*calling*) Bridget! (*She returns to the table and picks up her glass*)

Bridget Clancy appears at the open door. She is about forty, an Irishwoman who passes as a "good sort", but who can quickly become abusive and aggressive. Drink is never far away from her

Clancy There's only old Bolders to serve out there.
Leila She can manage for a moment. (*She is trying to control herself*) That girl. You told her to come in here?
Clancy (*nodding*) Said she wanted to see you.
Leila You know very well she merely wanted a room. You could have told her there was nothing.
Clancy (*with an unpleasant grin*) Not the boss, am I?
Leila Now look here, it's not part of your job to discuss my private affairs with every stranger who walks in.
Clancy How could I be doing that? I don't happen to know nothing about your private life.
Leila Then how did that young woman know about my daughter?
Clancy (*insolently*) Oh—that. 'T'isn't what you'd be calling classified information.
Leila (*losing control*) It's nothing to do with her or you!
Clancy You finished? 'Cos I've got a full bar out there.
Leila It can wait. (*She moves about restlessly before continuing*) For some time I haven't liked your attitude, Clancy.
Clancy (*heavily*) Mrs Clancy.
Leila All right—Mrs Clancy, Mrs Bridget Clancy! Look, you're a good worker and you know the job. I've been fair to you, but for some weeks you've gone out of your way to annoy me...

Clancy Sorry about that.
Leila You've got to admit it. I'm not saying anything about your deliberate rudeness, nor—(*she lets this out in an unguarded moment*)—about irregularities in the bar receipts...
Clancy (*quietly*) You watch it, missis.
Leila Well, it's true, and you know it. But young Trudi Bauer. I didn't take on a Swiss *au pair* girl for you to make a bosom friend of her. And it's not fair to her.
Clancy I didn't know I had leprosy.
Leila Oh, don't be a bloody fool. You're twice her age. Well, in a small village like this she can't get proper companions. But that's no excuse for you to take her out drinking and visiting the sort of people you know around here.
Clancy Ah, and I know some terrible people.
Leila I didn't say terrible. Downright unsuitable.
Clancy She's a fancy to visit Ireland, and who am I to stop her? Or you?
Leila You're always talking about Ireland. Perhaps it wouldn't be a bad idea if you went back to it—permanently.
Clancy It might come to that.
Leila Look, Bridget, there's no need for all this.
Clancy All this what?
Leila Oh—animosity! If you've a grievance, out with it. But don't go starting a campaign against me. I've always done my best to treat you fairly...
Clancy Oh, you're a grand lady.
Leila (*ignoring it*) As for the Swiss girl, well, I have an obligation to her parents to keep her out of trouble.
Clancy An' trouble is me, is that what you're getting at?
Leila She's eighteen, a young Continental, who is not used to making rounds of pubs...

Clancy laughs

But, more than that, why on earth do you have to tell a complete stranger that I had a daughter away at boarding-school?
Clancy But I didn't, see?
Leila Don't play about; of course you did. (*She checks for a moment*) How else would she know?
Clancy Ah. Now, that's an interesting thought. How?
Leila (*regarding the other steadily*) You didn't volunteer the information?
Clancy I did not. She comes in like any other casual, orders liqueur brandy an' starts talkin' like she knew all about you.

Leila is plainly disturbed. She tries to cover this by collecting the glasses from the table

Leila Just some busybody. Well, let's hope that's the end of the matter. All right, Bridget, we'll forget all about it.

Act I, Scene 2   9

Clancy Oh, I'll forget it. 'T'isn't the important matter it seems to be to you.

To avoid further conversation, Leila returns the bottles to the cupboard

Clancy waits for a moment, then goes off to the bar

Leila closes the cupboard and goes slowly over to the desk. She starts to light a cigarette, then turns sharply

In the fading light, Ruth Cousins is standing looking in at the window

Leila jabs her cigarette down, goes quickly to the window, and opens it

Leila I've already warned you. This time I'm going to phone the police!
Cousins Want a bet?
Leila Keep away from here! What is it you want?
Cousins A room for the night. Or two nights, or three...

CURTAIN

SCENE 2

The same. The next morning

The room is empty. After a moment Mrs Bolders comes in from the bar. She is wearing a hat and pulling on her jacket. She goes across and opens the door L

Mrs Bolders (*calling*) I'm on my way, Mrs Markham! (*Returning, she finds a bottle of whisky and glasses on the desk. She takes them to the cabinet*)

Trudi Bauer enters L *with a tray of used breakfast things. She is a Swiss student, in her teens or just over. Her English is very good, with a definite accent*

Trudi Good morning, Mrs Bolders.
Mrs Bolders Mornin', m'dear. (*Staring*) Breakfast in bed? She ill?
Trudi (*resting the tray on the table*) Not Mrs Markham. The other lady.
Mrs Bolders What other lady you talkin' about?
Trudi I do not know her name. She stay night. I think she friend of Mrs Markham.
Mrs Bolders Must 'ave come late, 'cos I was here until... There's no room—'cept Debbie's.
Trudi She sleep there.

Leila enters L. *She is disturbed and her manner is short*

Mrs Bolders Mornin'.
Leila Good morning, Mrs Bolders. (*She glances at Trudi, who is still standing at the table*) Well, Trudi? We don't do the washing-up in here.

Trudi goes out to the bar with the tray

Mrs Bolders Seems you've had a visitor.

Leila affects not to hear. She takes some pound notes from the desk drawer

Leila I owe you for Thursday and Friday. (*She goes to her*)
Mrs Bolders Trudi says you had a guest for the night.
Leila (*shortly*) That's right.
Mrs Bolders It was never that young woman who was askin' in the bar?
Leila What?
Mrs Bolders That casual—woman what had the brandy.
Leila I don't know anything about that.
Mrs Bolders I mean, I wouldn't put the likes of 'er up in my cottage, not on no account.
Leila Mrs Bolders, put someone up for the night. That's all there is about it.
Mrs Bolders (*with a shrug*) If you says so.
Leila She was—she was in difficulties.
Mrs Bolders Must have bin. You got two bedrooms up there an' you've never let no-one sleep in Debbie's room...
Leila (*losing control for a moment*) Well, for once I did, and there's nothing more to be said!
Mrs Bolders (*looking at her curiously*) You all right?
Leila I—I have a bit of a headache.
Mrs Bolders Sorry. (*She puts the money in her bag and goes across to the bar door*) I mean, if you wants me to stay a bit an' do upstairs...?
Leila (*not taking it in*) Why upstairs, for heaven's sake?
Mrs Bolders (*with a shrug*) Bedroom bin slept in. You'll want it put straight.

Leila turns, is about to reply hotly, but checks

Leila Trudi can manage anything required.
Mrs Bolders Right. Be in this evenin' as usual.

Mrs Bolders goes off to the bar

Leila puts her hand to her head wearily. Catching sight of a glass Mrs Bolders has left on the table, she snatches it up and puts it in the cabinet

As Leila turns back, Ruth Cousins is standing by the door L

Act I, Scene 2

Cousins Morning.

Leila slams the cabinet door shut

Leila Are you ready to go?
Cousins I'm in no hurry. (*She saunters over to the window and stands looking out with her back turned*) Been a bit of a shock to you, hasn't it? (*Turning*) Still, you've had a whole night to get used to the idea.
Leila (*with an effort*) When you get the money that's the end of it.
Cousins Friendly bitch, aren't you? You'd think me knowing what I do, you'd loosen-up a bit. It doesn't work with me, you know, putting on the fall-guy act. And how about the money, seeing we're on that subject?
Leila I can give you two hundred now...
Cousins Not a chance.
Leila The rest within an hour or so.
Cousins Ah. Sent someone to get it from where you've salted it away?
Leila I tell you I have no money but what is my own!
Cousins (*with a laugh*) Come off it. When your bloke did the Kilburn job he pickled enough to keep you off the dole queue. What—fifty thousand?
Leila (*tersely*) When that happened I had already left my husband.

Cousins laughs disbelievingly

I knew nothing of his doings or his money.
Cousins Well, well. How come you get the ready to start this place? Saved out of the housekeeping? Do tell me; I like a laugh.
Leila If you must know, and I see no reason why I should tell you anything...
Cousins (*sharply*) We've been through that.
Leila I had a small legacy from an aunt.
Cousins Nice. (*She lights a cigarette and flops into the chair by the table*) Ever done porridge?
Leila If you mean, have I been to prison—no.
Cousins I wonder? 'T'isn't no holiday camp, but if you keeps your ears open you picks up some useful things. Like a bloke I shacked up with once. Did a stretch at Albany. Still doing it. Seems he was in a cell with a bloke—Arthur Robbins... You listening?
Leila (*chokingly*) No.
Cousins Well, you better bloody well had. Seeing that you're no Leila Markham. You're Mrs Arthur Robbins, wife of the one what did the big Kilburn job.
Leila Markham is my maiden name. I used it when I left my husband.
Cousins Sure. Plenty of cell-widows do that.
Leila (*with an effort*) Look, we've been through all this. By chance you've found out things about—about my past life. But it is past! I haven't seen Arthur Robbins for nearly four years, and I shall never see him again. I left him six months before that robbery and knew nothing about it...

Cousins Then how come you're handing over five hundred quid?

Leila stares at her

'Cos you're given to handouts and have taken a fancy to me? No, sister. Just because you know bloody well that one word from me about Mrs Arthur Robbins blows you an' your quiet country life right out in the cold.

There is a silence

Leila This money is the finish, you understand that?

Cousins You don't have to tell me how far I can go. Five hundred quid. 'T'isn't what you'd call a fair share of the Kilburn job. Only I know your type, sweetheart. Put the pressure on and you lose your cool and start crying blue murder. You're just lucky, that's all. 'Cos I'd screw you for ten thousand if I thought there was a chance of getting it.

Leila You'd be wasting your time, because I haven't got ten thousand.

Cousins No? Let's talk about five hundred. I'm not hanging around this cabbage-patch all day.

Leila goes to the desk and unlocks a drawer. She takes out a packet of notes and returns to the table

Leila Two hundred. The rest is coming.

Cousins When? When you've sauntered round to the bank?

Leila This is all I can get from the bank. Do you think I want you in this house a minute longer than is necessary? I'm borrowing the rest.

Cousins Who from? (*She shrugs as there is no reply*) All the same to me. (*She goes across to the drawer at the desk and pulls it open*) Okay. (*She then picks up a framed photo*) Ah, your kid. I've heard about her.

Leila grows taut

At a special boarding-school down in Sussex. Costs you a small fortune, don't it? Something more than a measly five hundred quid. Twice as much as that a year, I bet.

Leila She needs special care.

Cousins Reckon she does, with the ma and pa she's got.

Leila (*losing control*) Get out of my house! Do you hear? I'll meet you in the village and give you the rest there!

Cousins (*with quiet viciousness*) Okay. Okay; if you wants a shouting-match, I'm the one for you. Go on, we'll let everyone know all about you. (*She moves to the windows and throws them open*) Ready?

Leila drops into the chair by the table

Leila You're getting what you came for. But why do you have to be such a bastard?

Cousins 'Cos it matches up with the kind I meet. (*She flicks through the notes*) Where you getting the rest from?

Leila I told you. I'm borrowing it.

Cousins (*with a short laugh*) I believe you, thousands wouldn't. The bank?
Leila A neighbour.
Cousins M'm. Curious, weren't they?
Leila I said it was for an unexpected bill.
Cousins Unexpected, all right. Don't matter to me, you know, only you'd better pay 'em back quick an' stop any awkward thinking. (*She goes to door* R) I'll be back soon to see if the cash has turned up, so you'd better hurry it. I've a nasty trick of getting impatient, and then anything can happen. Oh, and I always fancy a drink about this time, so have it set up.

Cousins goes out to the bar

Leila rises wearily and closes the window

Trudi comes in from the bar

Trudi Mrs Markham, I go to the shops.
Leila (*absently*) What?
Trudi To get things we want. I think we are short of some groceries.
Leila I see. That's all right. (*She goes across and locks the drawer in the desk*) But surely the grocer calls this afternoon?
Trudi (*hesitating*) Yes—well, there are other things.
Leila Look, Trudi, if you want to go out for an hour or two, you don't have to invent excuses.
Trudi No. I am sorry.
Leila Surely I'm always pretty reasonable? If you've done your work, your time's your own.
Trudi Thank you. You are very good.
Leila Nonsense.
Trudi Thank you very much. (*She hurries to the bar door*)
Leila Trudi? I would like to know where you are going. Just for a walk?
Trudi Yes, for a walk.
Leila Or to meet someone?

Trudi stares

Surely you can tell me?
Trudi Yes—perhaps.
Leila Bridget Clancy?
Trudi Is there something wrong in that?
Leila What? Look, Trudi, I've worries of my own. You might say that your affairs are no concern of mine. Well, they aren't, except that I am responsible for you—to your parents.
Trudi You mean I do bad things?
Leila No, no. Well, unwise things. You are in a strange country for the first time...
Trudi You mean Bridget do bad things?

Leila I didn't say anything of the sort. Bridget is well enough for her personal friends and people who know her. But I'm certain she is no good to you.
Trudi Why, please?
Leila Oh, good heavens, girl, foreign or not, you must know something of people. She comes of a rough Irish family. She's a good worker and she can be amusing, but it ends there. You go to pubs with her, don't you?
Trudi Pardon?
Leila Public houses, hotels—drinking.
Trudi I drink in Switzerland.
Leila (*giving it up*) Oh! What's the use of talking?
Trudi And I like people when they are kind and friendly to me.
Leila I've warned you; that's all I have to say.
Trudi Yes, Mrs Markham.

Trudi exits to the bar

Leila drops into the chair by the table. She presses her fingers to her head

Minnie Akers appears at the window and knocks on the glass

Leila grows taut and sits staring in front of her. The knocking is repeated. Leila turns and sees who it is

Leila exits to the bar, and returns with Akers

Akers Sorry to peer in like that, but I didn't know where you might be.
Leila No need to apologize, Miss Akers; it's very good of you to come.
Akers Startled you, though, didn't I? Did you think it was that prowler?
Leila I'm a little—well, unsettled.
Akers Okay. (*She takes a packet of notes out of her carrier-bag*) Three hundred, wasn't it?
Leila What must you think of me?
Akers Don't have to think anything, do I? Have I ever been short of the ready? Oh, boy. There was a time once when I had the chance to snap up a Louis Quinze cabinet. Do you know, I scraped up bits from everyone—including the milkman. And that made the neighbours talk!
Leila I can arrange something with my bank in a week or two. But this sudden demand—to do with Debbie's boarding-school expenses...
Akers I don't want to know. Can't you understand that? I had the loose cash by me and it'll do more good with you than it will with me. Say a fortnight?
Leila Within a week. I shan't have a moment's peace until it's paid back.
Akers And I shan't have a moment's peace if it isn't.
Leila Miss Akers...!

Act I, Scene 2

Akers Oh, shut up; that's a joke. (*Regarding her*) Sure you're all right? You don't look so hot.
Leila Quite all right. I suppose I had a bad night, that's all.
Akers Worry about that daughter of yours, don't you?
Leila Sometimes. Oh, she's happy, and that's all that matters. But she does mean a terrible lot to me.
Akers You'd be a funny mother if she didn't. I'm the same, only about my old tortoise. (*Looking round the room*) Pity you haven't got anything worth selling. Could have chipped a bit off that three hundred if you had. (*Her casual roaming takes her up to the window*) One should always have something valuable tucked away. Useful when you want quick cash. And it keeps antique dealers alive. Hullo, there's that girl in the soppy cap still trailing around. Not coming here, is she?
Leila I—I shouldn't think so.
Akers Probably fancies a swig of brandy after her cornflakes. Bit cool the way she barged in here last night. Did you send her off with a flea in her ear?
Leila She—she went eventually.
Akers (*moving to the bar door*) Okay, then. Be seeing you. All right, all right; no need to see me out as if I were an oil sheikh.
Leila Miss Akers—I am terribly grateful.
Akers Had to say that, didn't you? Well, don't. I'll get it out of you—in gin.

Akers goes off to the bar

Leila puts the money into a drawer in the desk, then turns

Ruth Cousins is standing by the bar door

Leila How did you get in?
Cousins One went out, one came in.
Leila She saw you?
Cousins Obviously, unless the old bag is blind.
Leila You might try not to make things so difficult for me. I said nothing about your staying here. Now what will she think?
Cousins Can't say I'm worried what she thinks. (*Sitting in the chair by the table*) What she want here?
Leila She's a friend and neighbour. She loaned me the money.
Cousins Don't give me that.
Leila I told you I was borrowing it. Where do you think I got it from?
Cousins You tell me. The attic, or some outhouse. Maybe behind the beer barrels in the cellar.
Leila It's here. (*Turning to the desk*) Take it and go.
Cousins Hold it. I'm not being paid-off like I was the char or the laundry. We do it civilized like, see? You can pour me a drink.
Leila (*contemptuously*) Brandy, I suppose?

Cousins A large gin—straight.

Leila goes to the cabinet for a bottle and glass

(*Looking round*) Reckon you just can't wait to get out of this dump.
Leila This is my home and my living.
Cousins (*nodding*) Ah-ha?
Leila Yes. (*She goes to the desk and takes out the packet of notes*) And now be good enough to finish your drink, take the money and go. (*She throws the packet on the table*)
Cousins (*picking up the money*) Three hundred quid?
Leila With the two hundred you've had, five hundred. Final.
Cousins (*thrusting the notes into her pocket*) M'm.
Leila Aren't you going to count them?
Cousins Never bother about counting small change. (*She leans back in her chair and sips her drink*) Going to keep little Debbie short of pocket money, isn't it? Oh, come on. Kind of school she's at? Bet she doesn't get by on fifty pence a week. (*There is a silence as Leila stands there, tight-lipped*) Layham Court House? Bet the girls there keep their own cheque books in their gym-lockers——
Leila (*in a burst*) How did you know that?
Cousins Know what?
Leila The name of the school?
Cousins Ah, well . . .
Leila (*desperately*) Nobody could know. Not even your precious cronies in prison!

Cousins laughs and leans over to pour herself out another drink

How did you know?
Cousins Kids at boarding-schools have suitcases and trunks—with labels on them. Simple.
Leila Clancy! My woman in the bar.
Cousins Puts the booze away a bit, doesn't she? That always oils the tongue.
Leila And you've been using it to get information out of her!
Cousins You know, sister, you lose your cool too much for someone who plays your sort of game.
Leila (*quietly*) Get out.
Cousins I'm going. One night in this crummy joint is enough for me. (*She gets up and moves slowly over to the door* L)
Leila That's not the way out.
Cousins I've got a holdall up in the bedroom. Don't want me to leave it behind as a keepsake, do you? Mind you, I could pick it up next time I come.
Leila (*catching her breath*) Next time?
Cousins Sure. Say for the second instalment? Five hundred doesn't last me all that long.

Act I, Scene 2

Leila stands for a moment staring at the other, then she goes over to her

Leila (*firmly*) You'd better get this straight. You think I've got money hidden away here and that you can keep coming back for more. Well, I haven't. So if you come here again it'll be for the last time. You'll not blackmail me any further. That's right! (*She moves quickly to the window*) I'll open this window—just as you did yesterday—and let everyone know the truth. You'll not bleed me.

Cousins (*after regarding the other for a while*) Okay. It was worth a try, anyway.

Cousins goes off L

Leila puts her hand to her head as she thinks. Then she goes quickly to the telephone and dials a number

Leila (*on the phone*) Layham Court House? . . . This is Mrs Markham. I would like to speak to Miss Alexander. . . . Oh, it's you, Miss Alexander. It's—it's just about Deborah. She is well? . . . Oh, good. Look, this is rather on the spur of the moment, but I might like to take her away for a few days. . . . Yes, a very short holiday. Do you think that would be possible? I know it is in the middle of term, but . . . Yes, it is rather important or I wouldn't have suggested it—— (*She senses that someone is in the room. She turns her head quickly*)

Bridget Clancy is leaning against the bar door, a cigarette in her mouth

Well, if you'll think about it, I'll phone you back this evening. . . . Yes, this evening. (*She drops the receiver and gets up quickly*) What are you doing here? It's an hour to opening time.

Clancy (*speaking thickly and giving every appearance of having been drinking*) Let's say I've opened the bar already.

Leila Then you'd no right to! And you've been drinking.

Clancy S'right. (*She catches sight of the bottle on the table and lurches towards it*) An' now you an' me's goin' to have a farewell drink. (*She slops the gin into the glass*)

Leila You'll leave my employ—now!

Clancy Ah, shut up. (*She drops into the chair by the table*) I'll be the one'll be sayin' that sort of thing. (*Nodding*) I'll be in Limerick this time tomorrow.

Leila Good.

Clancy (*with an ugly laugh*) Thought you'd be seein' it like that, Mrs Markham—or whatever your name is. (*Looking round the room*) Where's your visitor? Hurrying to the bank with the five hundred pounds you gave her?

Leila stands staring at her

Nice, eh? She gets a fat handout while I work my bloody fingers off for what you chooses to give me. (*She jerks herself out of the chair*) Well, shall I tell you somethin'? I'm after a little bit for myself. How's that?

Leila You'll get the wages owing to you and nothing else.

Clancy Is that so? You talk fine for the wife of a jail-bird, Mrs Leila Markham! An' who's to know you've never been inside yourself?

Leila Get out of here!

Clancy You don't frighten me. I know too much about you, my lovely.

Leila You know nothing . . .

Clancy Ah, but I do. About bank robberies an' changed names, an' the fat money it takes to keep an idiot kid at a special school. Ah, poor little Debbie . . .

Leila (*with barely controlled emotion*) Don't you dare breathe her name . . .

Clancy I know the bell to ring, Mrs Markham. So if you don't like it . . . Well, I've a fancy to take a thousand pounds back to Ireland with me . . .

Leila I have no money!

Clancy Get it. Go on, get what I'm askin' for. (*She picks up the bottle by the neck and takes a step forward*) I mean business, missis, so don't make no mistake.

Leila No!

Clancy smashes the bottle against the table and presents the shattered base

Clancy It's the money or I change the look of your face!

Leila reels back against the desk

In that drawer, eh? Well, open it. If you don't, little Debbie isn't goin' to bear lookin' at her mammy.

Clancy makes another step forward. On an impulse, Leila pulls open the drawer and gropes inside, taking out the revolver

Leila (*levelling the revolver*) I'm warning you, Clancy!

Clancy lurches forward, bottle raised. Leila fires twice, and Clancy checks and slumps down. Leila stares at her as if mesmerized

The door L opens and Cousins comes in. She stares at the scene, then goes over and kneels down by Clancy

Cousins (*staring at the blood on her hand*) You bloody fool. You've hurt her—bad.

CURTAIN

ACT II

The same. Early evening

The room is empty. The bar is open, so some noise is heard when the bar door is opened. Leila comes in R. *She is obviously under strain, and sits at the table. Mrs Bolders enters* R

Mrs Bolders You're not well, you know.
Leila (*getting up impatiently*) All right, all right. It's not helping having people follow me about and talking about it.
Mrs Bolders Sorry.
Leila I'm—I'm a bit run-down, that's all.
Mrs Bolders Just the point, ain' it? Look, it's only just gone half-past six. You could have a couple of hours on the bed afore we gets to the busy time ...
Leila No.
Mrs Bolders Fred from the village's here. Me an' 'im can manage them we gets in early evenin' ...
Leila All right, Mrs Bolders, and thank you. I shall be fine if I just sit down for half an hour.
Mrs Bolders Far from fine you look. Oh, just you wait 'til I sees that Clancy! Lettin' you down without so much as sendin' a word. What could have happened?
Leila (*turning away*) We don't know, do we? (*She stares down at the telephone as though half expecting it to ring*)
Mrs Bolders Oh, she won't phone, not 'er. Bet she's laughin' every time she thinks of us runnin' round in circles.
Leila (*automatically*) We don't know, we don't know. (*She stands with her back turned*)
Mrs Bolders I reckon she's gone back to Ireland. Fact, I'd take a bet she has. The last few days she's talked about nothin' else.
Leila (*getting it out with difficulty*) Perhaps.
Mrs Bolders Well, if she 'as, a damn good riddance, I say.

Trudi comes in L, *and stands by the door*

Anyhow, I'd better get back.

Mrs Bolders goes off to the bar

Leila makes a pretence of tidying the desk

Trudi Mrs Markham ...?

Leila (*not stopping what she is doing for fear of what may be said*) Yes, Trudi?
Trudi I could help in the bar.
Leila What? Oh, no.
Trudi Why not? I know what to do. Not perhaps to give drinks, but I could help.
Leila (*moving away from the desk*) No, dear. I appreciate your offer, but I assured your parents you would not be used on the business side. It's just—just a temporary situation.
Trudi (*anxiously*) You believe Bridget will come tomorrow?
Leila How can I say? Yes, yes; I expect so. We must wait and see, mustn't we?
Trudi People are taken ill. But Bridget never seemed the kind of person...

The phone bell rings. Leila stares across and then goes quickly to the desk

Leila (*on the phone*) Yes? (*She tries to conceal her concern*) Who is that speaking?...

Trudi moves above the desk, her hopes raised

I don't quite understand.... No, no; you have got the wrong number. (*She slams the receiver down*)
Trudi Not Bridget?
Leila (*losing control for the moment*) No, no; it was not Bridget! (*Moving away from the desk*) When I know, you'll know. And I don't see what particular concern it is of yours. I'm sorry, Trudi. (*Abruptly*) I'm going to the bar.

Leila exits R

Trudi stands there, then she goes to the door R *and opens it a few inches to make sure that Leila has gone. She goes quickly to the desk and dials a phone number*

Trudi (*on the phone*) The *White Hart*?... Please, is Mr Guthrie there?... Oh, Mr Guthrie, it is Trudie Bauer.... Yes, from *The Hay Wain*.... Please tell me if Bridget Clancy has been in.... No? This morning I wait for her at your hotel for an hour.... I see; she has not been in all the day. Thank you. (*She replaces the receiver and moves slowly away from the desk, visibly disturbed. Reaching the table, she bangs on it with her clenched fist*) Was kann ich fur sie tun!

The front doorbell rings

At first Trudi is hardly aware of it, then she goes out through the bar, leaving the door open. A moment later she returns with Beryl Fountain

Fountain (*as she enters*) Busy in the bar? Well, that's all right. I've only called with the receipt for her subscription.

Act II

Trudi Mrs Clancy has not come this evening. It makes her... (*groping for the word*)
Fountain Shorthanded. Oh, poor Mrs Markham. She could do without trouble like that. Mrs Clancy ill?
Trudi We hope so.
Fountain (*with a laugh*) Well, that's nice.

The bar door opens quickly, and Leila stands there. She had expected Cousins, and her disappointment shows

Leila Mrs Fountain.
Fountain Brought your receipt, that's all. Not stopping, my dear; I've heard how you're placed.
Leila All right, Trudi; just give a hand with the glasses. Nothing else.

Trudi goes off through the bar

Fountain (*putting the receipt on the table*) Hear your Irish firebrand has let you down. Well, you always stuck up for her, but she was never my type. What's her excuse?
Leila We've heard nothing.
Fountain H'm. What you going to do if she doesn't come back?
Leila (*with an effort*) I hadn't thought, Mrs Fountain.
Fountain Oh, well, as long as it doesn't throw more on you. You're looking quite done-up enough as it is.

The front doorbell rings. Leila grows taut

Fountain I'll be off. 'Bye-'bye.
Leila No—just a moment. (*Going quickly to the bar door*) There was something I wanted to ask...

Leila goes off, closing the door behind her

Fountain wanders aimlessly towards the window and looks out

Leila returns, followed by Minnie Akers

It was only Miss Akers.
Akers Only? Who did you expect—Mickey Mouse? (*Seeing Fountain*) Oh—you.
Fountain I'm off. (*To Leila*) What was it you wanted to ask me?
Leila Ask...?
Fountain When the doorbell rang. You stopped me from going.
Leila (*confused*) Oh... (*Putting her hand to her head*) I can't think what it was...
Fountain She's played out. And on the top of it, that Irishwoman hasn't turned up.

Leila moves away to the desk

I think she'd appreciate it if we cleared off.
Akers (*nodding*) Sure. (*She moves to the bar door*) Don't really know why the hell I came. Oh, yes. I ran across that woman of yours this afternoon . . .

Leila turns sharply. Can she possibly mean Clancy?

You know—the one who barged in here. The one with the cap.
Leila (*barely audibly*) Oh. Where?
Akers In Dorchester. Having lunch. At a pretty pricey place, too.
Leila Dorchester? You're sure of that?
Akers I've got eyes.
Leila (*with little control over her words*) But that's a long way from here.
Akers A good sixteen miles.
Fountain (*a little impatiently*) Surely it isn't all that important? A young woman we saw yesterday has lunch in Dorchester. So what?
Akers So nothing. Only it looks as though she is out of Mrs Markham's hair. Thought you'd like to know.
Leila Thank you. Yes—thank you. (*She is far from reassured. As she aimlessly rearranges things on the desk, she knocks a photo frame to the floor*)
Fountain (*quietly*) Come on. (*She goes to the bar door*) See you sometime, my dear.

Fountain goes off

Akers hesitates for a moment, and regards Leila, who is picking up the photo frame

Akers follows Fountain off

Leila slowly rises and drops the photo frame on the desk, then moves slowly towards the table

Leila (*in despair*) Oh, God!

The door opens, and Akers stands there

Leila, rooted, stares at her

(*At last*) Don't spy on me!

Akers closes the door quietly. She goes to the cabinet and takes out the brandy bottle and a glass. Leila feels for the chair by the table and drops into it. Akers pours out some brandy, puts the glass in front of Leila and sits in the chair below the desk

Akers Drink it. (*Sharply*) Drink it!

Act II

Leila reaches out for the glass and drinks

Better? Well, what's all this about?
Leila (*after draining the drink*) Nothing.
Akers Only idiots appeal to the Almighty about nothing.
Leila I'm worried about the business. Can't you understand!
Akers You're worried about a damned sight more than that. (*Sharply*) Come on!

Leila jerks herself out of the chair and moves up to the windows

You can tell me, you know. And if you don't tell somebody, you'll crack-up. That'll be worse, won't it?
Leila (*her back turned*) You heard me say something. Well? Everyone says something on an impulse.
Akers (*quietly*) Not the way you said it. And how about the "spying" bit? Not the kind of thing one says about one's friendly next-door neighbour.

Leila turns her head slowly and looks at her

Now, if it had been Fountain . . . Well, she's a J.P. and copper-bottomed. I'm half way to being a bit of a crook.
Leila That's absurd.
Akers Oh, I've done some mildly shady things with reproduction furniture. Yes, and kept my thumb over the E.P.N.S. mark. But yours is a bit more, isn't it? Oh, come on! Don't be a clot. I keep my eyes and ears open, you know. (*She moves up to Leila*) There's something between you and that bloody girl who walked in here yesterday. Isn't there?

Leila looks at her, then turns and drops into the settee

Leila Miss Akers—I'm in ghastly trouble!
Akers I guessed that. Just how ghastly?
Leila Can I trust you? (*With emphasis*) Really trust you?
Akers You've got to chance that.
Leila (*in a burst*) It's about that young woman and—(*her voice drops*)—Clancy. The woman—her name is Cousins—knows a man who is in prison with my husband.

She expects Akers to say something, but there is no sign

I left my husband over three years ago, because I found out—soon after he was convicted of the Kilburn bank robbery. (*She goes on a little wildly*) My proper name is Robbins. Wife of a criminal. My whole life here is a lie . . .! (*She stops and leans her head against the back of the settee*)

Akers goes to the table, pours out some more brandy and returns. Leila feels the glass touching her hand and drinks

Akers (*quietly*) And this woman?

Leila She thinks I have the stolen money that was never found.
Akers But you haven't.
Leila No! No! I told her. I left my husband before any of it happened!

Akers goes quietly to the cabinet and pours herself out a gin

Akers Blackmailing you, is she?
Leila I've paid her five hundred pounds.
Akers That was why you borrowed that money from me.
Leila Yes.
Akers Then you're a damned fool. Don't you know that sort of thing is only just the beginning?
Leila Of course I know. And if it hadn't been for my fears for providing for Debbie I wouldn't have done it.
Akers (*impatiently*) Providing for Debbie? And how are you going to do that if you have to keep this bitch going with handouts? Eh? From the bar profits? Next time she comes for cash, tell her it's finished. You'll have to. Oh, maybe she'll see it's no good and leave you alone. But you've got to tell her.
Leila (*bitterly*) Do you think I haven't already told her that? I have. Told her it was finished. Just as my pleasant life here is finished . . .
Akers Cobblers. Decent people won't care a rap.
Leila You don't know it all! It was like that—until Clancy came.
Akers Clancy?

With an effort Leila rises and turns on the lights, then moves towards the table. Having told something of her trouble, she has found a new strength

Leila (*without emotion*) She came in here this morning—drunk. She shouted at me, said she knew as much about my past as that woman did. She, too, wanted money, and when I refused she came at me with a broken bottle. You'll never believe this, Miss Akers. I was frightened, desperate, but all the time I thought only of Debbie . . . I shot her. (*She drops into the chair by the table*)
Akers That pistol you keep in the desk? How badly?
Leila I don't know. She was bleeding—holding her shoulder. That woman took her to a hospital in my car.

Akers moves up slowly and looks towards the window

Akers When was this?
Leila This morning. Eleven, twelve—I don't know.
Akers And what have you heard since?
Leila Nothing.
Akers Nothing?
Leila Nothing, nothing! (*She makes an effort to get up but sinks back*) No phone—nothing. Can you imagine what it's been like expecting every moment to have news of some sort? Six hours—more, and nothing. At least it gives one some idea of what hell is like.
Akers (*coming down*) Look, I told you I saw her in Dorchester. Clancy

couldn't have been badly hurt. Would a woman—even that woman—go and calmly eat lunch in an hotel if she had serious trouble on her hands?
Leila I don't know.
Akers (*insisting*) Would she? All right, you don't know, and it's six hours since she went off. We know nothing. But I wouldn't mind betting she dumped Clancy at the nearest hospital with a flesh wound and made the hell out of it.
Leila Keeping my car?
Akers (*with a shrug*) What do you think?
Leila She would have to explain how she found Clancy like that...
Akers I reckon she's the sort who could explain anything. Did you see where you hit her?
Leila I told you. She was holding her shoulder. She was bleeding badly, because that woman had to more or less carry her to the car. (*Wearily*) What do I do now?
Akers Sit tight. Don't start dragging the police into it. Not unless it becomes necessary. If anyone has to press charges against you it's Clancy. And from what you've told me she's hardly likely to do that. As for that young woman, I don't think you'll see her again. They've drawn blanks, both she and Clancy.
Leila (*getting up, a little reassured*) Thank you. I don't know what I should have done without you.
Akers Something bloody silly, you bet. You all right now?
Leila Not quite so hopeless.
Akers Good. (*Going to the bar door*) I'll look you up later tonight—when the bar's closed. In the meantime, try and do some work out there. As far as you are concerned everything's the same as it always has been.
Leila Is it? You forget one thing, Miss Akers. I'm not the woman you thought I was. I'm the wife of a convicted bank robber.
Akers Are you? Oh, yes. Bad luck. Still, I reckon you'll get over it.

With an encouraging nod, Akers goes off to the bar

Leila looks round the room. She has found something of a new strength. She returns the glasses to the cabinet. Then she goes to the bar door and opens it

Leila (*calling*) Mrs Bolders! (*She returns to the room*)

Mrs Bolders comes in

How are things out there?
Mrs Bolders Easy enough. Most of the early drinkers have gone, and there's only two or three.
Leila Good. And has Trudi been useful?
Mrs Bolders Oh, yes—the odd things. Wish she didn't like doin' it, though. An' that's Clancy's fault...

Leila (*dismissing it*) Yes, yes. I'll be out there in a moment, so if you'd like to go off...
Mrs Bolders No, I wouldn't. What, with the busy time comin' up? T'is Saturday, you know. I'm stayin'.
Leila All right, Mrs Bolders, and thank you very much.
Mrs Bolders Don't have to thank me for nothin'. Only just you sees you give it hot an' strong to that Clancy.

Mrs Bolders goes off to the bar

Leila stands for a moment taking a breath as she collects herself. She goes to the mirror on the cabinet, examines her face and tidies her hair. Then, sensing someone is in the room, she turns sharply

Ruth Cousins is standing in the doorway L

Leila How—how did you get in?
Cousins Window in the passage. Did you want me to walk in through the front door where everyone could see me? (*She has lost her early insolent composure, and she jerks her words out*) Get me a drink. (*She closes the door*)
Leila I want to know what happened...
Cousins I said get me a drink!

As Leila turns to the cabinet Cousins drops into the chair by the table

Leila (*bringing a bottle and glass to the table*) I've been waiting hours—six hours! And you didn't even trouble to phone and tell me...

Cousins makes an impatient gesture for the drink

I've been at my wit's end. And you calmly go and have lunch at some hotel...
Cousins (*turning sharply*) How d'ye know that?
Leila You were seen. Miss Akers happened to be in Dorchester. Does it matter?
Cousins It matters if you've been shooting-off your mouth. Don't tell me you've been such a crazy fool as to tell anyone?
Leila No! It came out by chance. She happened to see you and mentioned it casually.

Cousins looks at her carefully, then drains her glass

Cousins I've done a few things in my life but I hit the jackpot when I got lumbered with you.
Leila (*desperately*) I want to know about Clancy!
Cousins 'Spose you do. She's dead.

Leila stares unbelievingly

(*Jerking herself out of the chair*) Got me caught up in something fine,

Act II

haven't you? A woman who keeps a gun in a drawer and shoots someone down in cold blood!
Leila (*shaking her head as she stares at the other*) I don't—I don't believe it.
Cousins (*with low emphasis*) I tell you she's dead. If you don't believe me, go and look at her.
Leila (*almost inaudibly*) Where is she?

Cousins does not answer, but goes to the table and pours out another drink

Cousins I got her to the car all right—didn't seem too bad. She was holding her shoulder. Drove her to the doctor you gave me. Seemed the chances were reasonable—accident with a gun, cleaning it—anything. I tell you during the drive she actually spoke. (*She finishes her drink before continuing*) After a couple of miles I heard her slump on to the floor of the car. Fired twice, you told me. Didn't you!
Leila Yes, yes! I fired twice.
Cousins You must have got her in the ribs.
Leila (*quietly*) I see. Well, I know what I have to do now. (*She goes slowly to the desk*)
Cousins Do what?
Leila Phone the police.
Cousins Hold it. (*She goes over and stands above the desk*) There's a bit more you'd better hear. Do you think I was going to drive around like that? Come back to this place with a corpse for a passenger? Any moment I could have been stopped—cop check, someone asking the way. It was all right for you, sitting here while someone else does the dirty work! You might as well know. I've put her in a safe place.
Leila (*staring*) What do you mean?
Cousins What I say. Half a mile or so from here there's building work going on, in a lane just off the main road. Being Saturday there was no-one about—you listening?

Leila makes no sign, but stares ahead

Near the site there's the beginning of an old well-shaft...
Leila (*bursting out*) What are you saying?
Cousins She's there.
Leila Buried there? Just as though I were a murderer...!
Cousins (*viciously*) Aren't you? (*She moves quickly away to the table area, looking down at her shaking hand and then going on quietly but with an effort*) Get this, Mrs Markham, Mrs Robbins, or whatever you like to call yourself. I didn't mess myself up in this for your sake. Whether she lived or died, it would have come out. Clancy wasn't the one to let you get away with what you did to her. It would have come out, your past, the five hundred quid. All blown. And I wasn't going to have that. What's Clancy to you and me? Less than nothing. But don't forget one thing. You shot her and you're the one who'll take the rap.
Leila (*after standing for a moment with closed eyes*) Very well. She attacked

me, and I shot her in self-defence. I thought she was being taken to a doctor—but I didn't do this horrible thing you're talking about...

Cousins (*sharply*) All right. (*She goes above the desk and lifts the phone receiver*) Here's the phone. Out with the whole story. But don't forget it was *your* car she was taken away in.

Leila My car?

Cousins Have I got a car? No. (*She takes a car key from her pocket and holds it up*) You got a short memory. These are the keys you gave me this morning. So, you see, I didn't take Clancy's body out in your car. You did.

Leila No!

Cousins The car's outside. With bloodstains on the seat and on the floor. I know nothing about it. I was in the room upstairs packing up to go. Oh, yes, I heard what could have been a couple of shots, but I thought it was a tyre-burst out in the road. I know nothing, and it won't matter how much you swear I did.

Leila The police have got to be told!

Cousins Sure. Still, it's bad luck on your kid. She won't have a mother for fifteen or twenty years. And all because you was in too much of a hurry to blow everything.

Leila (*after a pause*) Put it down.

Cousins (*replacing the receiver*) You can get out of this if you go about it in the right way.

Leila Why did you have to come here!

Cousins Oh, come on! Clancy went for you with a bottle. She'd've done that whether I was here or not.

Leila (*wearily*) I suppose so.

Cousins (*going to the table and filling two glasses*) Be fairer to that kid of yours if you used a bit of sense. Who's worth considering, your daughter or that drunken Mick? (*She thrusts a glass into Leila's hand*) Clancy's gone back to Ireland.

Leila How can you say that?

Cousins (*quietly*) Gone back to Ireland. Just like she always said. She told me, a stranger; she's told you and everyone else. Right—she's gone.

Leila It's madness.

Cousins Suit yourself. Only don't forget I know nothing.

Leila drops into the chair by the table

Leila Leave her—leave her there?

Cousins nods

It's horrible.

Cousins So's fifteen years in stir. And you were only defending yourself, weren't you?

Leila I can tell the police that.

Cousins The police! Tell 'em what? Tell 'em something they won't believe? We've been through that.

Act II

Leila gets up and goes to the window. Then she turns

Leila They'll find her.

Cousins As she is now—yes. She's just covered with leaves and branches. But if I go out there tonight and finish the job properly, you can quit worrying.

With an involuntary movement Leila turns her back and faces the window

Far as you know, has she got any relations over here? (*She waits*) I asked you a question.

Leila No. She came here on her own a few months back. Some friends in the village.

Cousins People go off without telling friends. See my line, don't you? Clancy could go away from this place and no-one would ask questions.

Leila (*half turning*) The Swiss girl. They were fairly close.

Cousins So what? (*Going over to Leila*) Look, did she live in?

Leila She had a room over the kitchen.

Cousins (*in relief*) Now, that does help. You'll have to go over it for letters. Pack up her things and get them out of that room. Where's that gun?

Leila What? I don't know. (*She moves slowly away from the desk*)

Cousins You're a fine one. (*She pulls open a desk drawer, looks inside and then closes the drawer*) That can stay there, but pray hard no-one will want to come and look at it. Next thing is your car—stains and all that. All right, it'll be safe enough in the garage for a bit, but it mustn't be left like that. (*Going towards the door* L) I'll get it inside now.

Leila grips the arms of the chair by the table and bends over it

Better pull yourself together, hadn't you? Because one slip from you and I do like I said. See? I know nothing about all this and you carry the can yourself.

Leila (*making an effort and straightening up*) I'll be all right.

Cousins You'd better. And one thing more. I've come back and you're allowing me to stop for the weekend. Understand?

Leila nods

Now get a drink inside you and start acting normal

Cousins goes off L

Leila goes to the table, reaches for the bottle, then pushes it aside. She goes to the desk and stands looking down at the phone. The sight of her daughter's photo makes her realize the consequences of any action

Trudi enters from the bar

Trudi Mrs Markham?

Leila Yes? (*She moves up to pull the curtains at the window. It has the effect of calming her*) Yes, Trudi?
Trudi I think I have done all I can in the bar.
Leila I see. Thank you for your help.
Trudi I go out. If you do not object.
Leila No, no; of course not. (*Moving away*) When you're free your time is your own.
Trudi I have written to my mother. I would like to post the letter.
Leila Of course. (*Feeling she has to say something*) It's Saturday, though; you won't catch the post.
Trudi (*a little doggedly*) But I would like it to go.
Leila Then post it, girl, post it. The walk will do you good after that stuffy bar.
Trudi (*going to the window and looking out*) Oh, it is raining quite hard.
Leila Is it?
Trudi Yes. Mrs Markham, I know you don't like me asking, but have you heard anything from Bridget?
Leila What?
Trudi Bridget Clancy. It has been all day. I think she must have telephoned you.
Leila (*moving to the desk and doing some aimless tidying*) No—no, I haven't heard.
Trudi Why has she not come back? Not telephoned, not told anyone?
Leila My dear girl...
Trudi Mrs Bolders say she has gone back to Ireland. She wouldn't do that, would she?
Leila Trudi—how can I say? Of course, she was not—not contented here. It is always possible...
Trudi (*in a strange little outburst*) She wouldn't do it!
Leila (*with an effort*) I'm sorry, my dear, but I can't discuss the—the plans of people employed here. You have your own affairs to think about.
Trudi (*nodding, and with a strange emphasis*) Yes, I have.
Leila Well, run along—I have to go to the bar to help poor Mrs Bolders.

Trudi goes off to the bar

Leila is going to the mirror when the phone bell rings. She is tempted to ignore it, then she goes and picks up the receiver

Yes?... Oh—Miss Akers.... No—no, I've heard nothing. (*She tries to control her voice*) Nothing, I tell you.... All right, all right! Goodbye. (*She replaces the receiver*)

Ruth Cousins comes in L. She stands there stripping off a pair of gloves

Cousins Who was that?
Leila Nothing. A business call. Does it matter?

Act II

Cousins (*regarding her steadily*) No police nonsense?
Leila No! The brewers phoning me about an everyday thing. I've said, does it matter?
Cousins It better hadn't. You can pour me out a Scotch.

Leila goes to the cabinet. Cousins thrusts her gloves into her pocket and moves to the chair below the desk. She sits

Nice little job you've given me. Tinkering about in a garage at night. Wearing gloves, wiping off the outside so's I don't leave dabs on your car. And inside's not done yet. Later. Long as no-one comes along and is curious to look at the back seat. And we're hoping it won't come to that, aren't we?

Leila pours out a drink and brings the glass over

I hope you're grateful.
Leila You needn't pretend you're doing this for me!
Cousins You're dead right, chum; I ain't. I'm protecting Number One, good and hard. You see how your bloody quick temper has landed me, don't you? Accessory after the fact. That's not a thing you gets out of easy. (*Sipping the drink*) Soon as you gets that bar closed go up to her room and get rid of everything personal—clothes, suitcases, letters. Specially letters. (*With a slight laugh*) You were lucky picking someone with no tie-ups.
Leila People have been asking...
Cousins (*sharply*) Who?
Leila Mrs Bolders, my woman help.
Cousins (*dismissing it*) Ach.
Leila And the Swiss girl. They were friendly.
Cousins That don't mean a thing. No, the only ones who could stir things are relations, and all hers are tucked away in Guinness Land.
Leila I suppose so.
Cousins You start concentrating on what's important. Like the fact you've said I can stay on here for the weekend. You got to talk to people, like out there in the bar. It don't help if you go wandering about like a bloody ghost.
Leila There are limits to what I can stand.
Cousins (*getting up quickly*) Make up your mind. 'Cos if I thought for one moment you couldn't go through with it, I'd clear off now. This minute. And that leaves you to explain a body in an old well-shaft.
Leila I suppose such a thing as conscience doesn't mean a thing to you?
Cousins Don't preach cant to me! (*After a pause, she goes on quietly*) You got to think straight, chum. Conscience! You stops a drunken Mick from maiming you for life and you have to squeal because she's gone? Save your pity for that kid o' yours. She's the one who is going to suffer if you lose your nerve.
Leila (*recollecting*) For the weekend? Why do you have to stay here?
Cousins Why? Have some sense. There's that car to be cleaned up. Are

you going to do it? I can just see you! And not to mention a little job over at the building site. She's lying there covered with no more than leaves and twigs. It needs no more than the odd prowling dog to blow that lot. Someone's got to fill that hole for keeps.
Leila (*covering her ears*) I don't want to hear!
Cousins Do you think you can do without me?
Leila The weekend? When will you go?
Cousins When I'm satisfied. Like that you've got nothing to worry about and can concentrate on other things.
Leila Other things? You mean that money, don't you? The money I haven't got!
Cousins (*with a light laugh*) One thing at a time, chum. You don't have to start belly aching about money—not yet. Just hold hard to the fact that you're sitting on top of something that can blow you and your Debbie sky high. (*She drops into the sofa and leans back*) Get out in that bar and start acting like a proper landlady. Oh, and while you're there, see that that cupboard is stocked up. I don't want to have to blow a bugle every time I fancy a drink.

Leila stands irresolute for a moment, then goes quickly out to the bar

Cousins laughs softly, then gets up and pours out a drink. She takes the glass and lolls back in the settee. Then she becomes aware there is a tapping at the window. She lets it go, then gets up and parts the curtains an inch or two. Unable to see who it is, she pulls the curtains aside and opens the window

Outside, in a shaft of moonlight, is the figure of Clancy

You bloody fool! You're supposed to be in London! Do you want to blow everything?
Clancy (*quietly*) Depends, me darlin'. Got to talk about it, haven't we?

CURTAIN

ACT III

The same. The following Sunday morning

The room is empty, and from outside comes the sound of church bells. After a moment Trudi enters from the bar with a breakfast tray. As she goes across the room, Leila comes in L. *She is worried and distrait, and passes Trudi without a glance*

Trudi (*pausing at the door* L) The lady upstairs ask for breakfast. You were not here, Mrs Markham, so I hope I do the good thing.
Leila (*absently*) Yes, yes; of course.
Trudi It is Sunday morning and there is no-one else to cook. I do what I think is right.
Leila Yes, yes. All right, Trudi.
Trudi She ask for special breakfast. (*With a shrug*) I do the best I can . . .

The front doorbell rings. Leila grows taut

Leila Answer it, will you?

Trudi puts the tray on the desk and goes off through the bar

Leila moves up to the window and looks out

Trudi comes in from the bar with Minnie Akers. The latter carries a bag of golf clubs

Thank you, Trudi.

Trudi goes off L *with the tray*

Akers dumps her bag by the bar door

Akers Not for that woman?

Leila nods

Oh dear. That puts paid to my theory she wouldn't turn up again. Well, well. Look, I only brought this gear with me so that it would seem more normal. Everyone knows I play golf on Sunday morning. Sorry about last night, but I just couldn't get round. That's why I phoned. Well, what's she got to say for herself?

Leila turns sharply, her back to Akers

All right, I've given it plenty of thought, don't you worry. You've got to convince yourself it's all a big bluff. This woman happens to come in on this scene of yours with Clancy. So what does she do? Being a clever, unscrupulous bitch, she jumps at it as an opportunity to screw you for more money. And now she's got Clancy tucked up in some hospital, isn't that what she's selling you...?

Leila No! (*She turns slowly and faces Akers*) Clancy is dead.

There is a long pause. Leila drops into the chair near the table. Akers stands there looking at her, then she goes slowly towards the desk

Akers (*quietly*) How do you know that?
Leila How do you think! She told me, of course.
Akers I see. In some hospital?
Leila (*almost inaudibly*) No.
Akers No?
Leila (*with an effort*) She's never been near a hospital. Clancy—died during the journey. So that woman upstairs has put her somewhere in that building site off the Malling Road—covered with leaves and twigs. And now, now it's as you said it would be. She's talking about more money, and all because she did it for me. But nothing can alter the fact that Clancy is dead!

Akers regards her for a moment, then goes to the cabinet

I don't want drink. That's not going to help me now. Clancy is dead!
Akers (*sharply*) Shut up. That woman is upstairs. Do you want her to know you're telling all this to me?
Leila (*wearily*) What does it matter?

Akers moves up to the window. She is shocked at the news but still desperately seeking an explanation

Akers All right; all right. It's pretty grim stuff you're telling me. But that this woman would implicate herself in a shooting just to get more money... Look, if I'd been in her shoes I'd've got the hell out of it as soon as possible. (*Insisting*) You must see what I mean.
Leila I don't know. I suppose she thought she couldn't go to a hospital or a doctor and explain it all—panicked—something. (*Getting up*) But it doesn't alter the fact that that's what she's done.
Akers (*challenging*) Has she? (*She goes over to Leila*) How do you know all this? Because she told you. Such a good, honest, reliable friend. (*She moves away towards the bar door as she thinks it out*) Suppose at this very moment Clancy is not a mile from here, nursing a slight flesh wound? Well, did she tell you exactly where she had done this—burying?

Akers breaks off as she hears a noise on the stairs. She affects to be examining a club from her golf-bag

Trudi comes in L. *She pauses as though about to say something, but seeing Akers there she goes off to the bar*

Act III

Well, did she?
Leila Did she what?
Akers Tell you exactly where she had put her? I bet she didn't. Just left it vague, so there'd be no point in you checking...
Leila No! In an old well-shaft at the building site.

Akers looks at her for a moment, then goes slowly up to the window

Akers (*slowly, as she turns*) I don't believe it. What has she told you to do? Say nothing? Eh? Just let it be thought Clancy has gone home to Ireland?

Leila nods

She would. (*She moves down towards the desk*) The car she took her away in—yours?
Leila She hasn't a car.
Akers So if you go to the police, do anything but play along with her, she'll swear she knows nothing about it. Right?
Leila (*with an effort*) Miss Akers, you've been a good friend. Thank you. But now you know everything, and it's your duty to—well, to tell others...
Akers Don't waste time telling me about my duty.
Leila Then I beg you—please, I beg you—forget everything I've told you. It's more than I have any right to ask, but if you don't... The only thing that matters to me now is Debbie.
Akers If I say nothing, you intend to go along with the blackmail?
Leila I have no choice.
Akers (*nodding*) Good.

Leila stares at her

Go along with it. Go even further. This stolen money she believes you have hidden away—make her think you have it.
Leila I have no money!
Akers All right. But make her think you have. Because what we have to buy now is time. Make out you have it hidden away somewhere. Do anything that can give me time to get over to that building site and find out the truth!
Leila You don't believe Clancy is dead, do you? Despite all this woman has told me...
Akers (*with emphasis*) Because of what this woman has told you. God help me, I may be wrong, in which case you've got to be prepared for the worst. But I feel it in my bones that it's all too glib and simple to be just swallowed. (*She thinks she hears someone upstairs and moves over towards the door* L) I can be at that building site in minutes in the car. That's the only way we'll know for certain.
Leila You mean what you said? Pretend to her I have that money?
Akers Yes. Stall, play for time, but give her the impression you've got it somewhere.

Leila I doubt if I have the strength.

Akers (*sharply*) Then borrow some. (*Moving away from the door*) She's coming. (*She stands at the desk pretending to examine a small silver salver*)

Cousins enters L and stands watching Akers

Who told you it was George the Second? (*She slips a glass from her pocket and examines the salver*) People should know their markings before they start shooting off their mouths. It's Anne or King Billy, that's for sure. (*She looks up for a moment and nods to Cousins*) 'Morning. A nice little piece and it's William the Third. (*With a laugh*) If I weren't a damned fool, I'd try and tell you it was Victoria, but you can't fight hall marks. (*Putting the glass away*) Want to sell it? All right, I'm not rushing you, but I know a buyer who'd give something worth having.

Leila (*impelled to say something*) Thank you.

Akers Don't thank me; I'll get my whack if you do sell. (*Going to her golf bag*) From what I've seen of your place you've got some tidy little bits and pieces tucked about. Of some value, anyway. Treasures in the attic, eh? (*She shoulders the bag and goes to the bar door*) Heads I go to church, tails I play golf. I'll let you know who wins.

Akers nods and goes off to the bar

Cousins lights a cigarette and examines the salver as she leans against the desk

Cousins Of some value, eh? So you're not so blooming skint as you try and make out. As if I didn't know it. (*She jerks herself off the desk*) You been upstairs like I told you?

Leila Where?

Cousins Clancy's room—over the garage, wherever it is. You've had time enough to get rid of all her stuff.

Leila I—I'll do it this afternoon.

Cousins (*menacingly*) You'll do it . . . !

Leila I have to open the bar at twelve. This afternoon there'll be no-one about.

Cousins (*regarding her for a moment*) Okay. But we're not taking any chances, see? It's got to look like she's gone for good. (*She moves up to the window and looks out*) A Sunday morning and all quiet and peaceful. But I'm not for hanging on in this crummy joint. Not for one minute longer than necessary. Got that?

Leila I don't understand.

Cousins Don't give me that. You understand all right. You've got me caught up in a nasty bit of aggro and if I'm to save you from stir, I got to be paid—handsome.

Act III

Leila I tell you . . .
Cousins (*viciously*) And I tell you there's a stiff just a mile away from here what you shot. What you took there in your own car. (*She pauses to let this sink in*) Don't try and bring me into it, 'cos I'll be miles away. Of course, if you've got any sense and see what's best for you and your kid, well—I just slips over there as it gets dark and finishes the job. Nobody'll ever find her, you can bet on that.

Leila moves up, as much as to conceal her conflicting thoughts as anything

Leila (*her back turned*) What do you want?
Cousins Ten thousand.
Leila I haven't got it! (*With an effort she faces the other*) Five.

Cousins stares at the other searchingly. A moment of relief shows on her face, for there had always been the possibility there was no money

Cousins Handy? No banks and all that?
Leila Cash. (*Quickly*) But not in the house.
Cousins Where?
Leila I'm not telling you. And it's five or nothing.
Cousins Buried in the garden? Someone minding it for you? All right! But I've got to know how long it'll take to get it.
Leila (*having found from somewhere a new, desperate strength*) Half-an-hour.
Cousins Okay. But I warn you not to play games, chum. 'Cos if you do, I'll see you flattened.

The front doorbell rings

Who's that?
Leila I don't know.
Cousins Get rid of 'em. And get cracking. Half-an-hour and no more.

Trudi comes to the bar door and admits Beryl Fountain. Trudi goes off

Fountain Good morning. (*She looks curiously across at Cousins*) Sorry to bother you on a Sunday morning, but I've been trying to catch up with Miss Akers.
Leila She called in for a moment on her way to golf.
Fountain Oh, I see. She seems rather elusive this morning. I wonder what made her call here? Usually nothing interferes with her golf, and that's the other side of the village.
Leila She just looked in to value a piece of silver I have——
Cousins (*breaking in*) Look, I want to get some cigarettes before I go off. (*Going to the bar door*) Anyway, I'll be back in half-an-hour.

Cousins goes off through the bar door

Mrs Fountain looks at the door through which Cousins has gone

Fountain Don't you sell cigarettes?
Leila What? Yes, of course I do. I suppose she wants newspapers, something else.
Fountain H'm. (*She moves up to the window*) A rather strange young woman, don't you think?
Leila (*throwing it off with a laugh*) She's a stranger, certainly.
Fountain I distinctly remember you being very short with her on Friday night. Since then she must have convinced you of being a suitable lodger.
Leila She is going off shortly and I doubt if I shall ever see her again.

Mrs Fountain is attracted by a noise outside. She looks out of the window as a car is heard leaving

Fountain If you were not here in this room, I would say that was your car driving away.
Leila (*with unnecessary sharpness*) Of course it's my car. I'm sorry to be so short, Mrs Fountain, but I don't feel that I have to explain . . .
Fountain Of course you don't. (*All the same, she looks as though she expects an explanation*)
Leila (*moving away to cover her embarrassment*) I know you're surprised at her being here. So was Miss Akers. I felt sorry for her. She is cut off in this part of the world without friends. As for the car—well, I said she could borrow it to go over to Dorchester and book in at an hotel.
Fountain I see, my dear. Rather foolish of her not to have done that yesterday when she was lunching there.

Leila looks at her a little wildly. It is obvious Mrs Fountain will not be satisfied by any explanation offered

And what a wicked waste of your petrol. Especially if she used your car yesterday.

Leila is saved by a knock at the bar door. She starts to move towards it

Mrs Bolders enters

Mrs Bolders Oh—sorry.
Leila What is it, Mrs Bolders?
Mrs Bolders Sunday mornin', isn't it? I bin comin' here to wash an' clean-up for the past six months . . .
Leila Yes, yes; of course. You'll have to excuse me, Mrs Fountain. We get such a pile-up after Saturday night, and I open again at twelve.
Fountain Of course; I quite understand. And it is obvious you have a lot on your mind this morning. (*Going to the bar door*) I know the way out.

Mrs Fountain exits

Mrs Bolders Well, I never. Must be somethin' special to make her miss church.

Act III

Leila Yes. Mrs Bolders, it's good of you to come . . .
Mrs Bolders Eh? 'Tis Sunday, m'dear.
Leila I know that. Look, would you mind very much if I put you off this morning? (*Going on quickly*) Trudi and I can manage the clearing-up . . .
Mrs Bolders You what? Have you taken a look at that public bar? An' I don't know no reason why I shouldn't do the job I always does . . .
Leila Trudi and I can do it. Just this Sunday, that's all. You see, I'm a bit worried about her, and I want her to be fully occupied. You know she's been moody and unsettled lately. Being really busy might help.
Mrs Bolders So what's to stop me an' her doin' it? You know you ain't well . . .
Leila I'm perfectly all right. It's for Trudi's sake.

Mrs Bolders stares at her stolidly

Mrs Bolders, I shall pay you, of course.
Mrs Bolders (*with a shrug*) You're the boss, m'dear. An' if that's how you wants it . . . (*Turning to the door*) Can't say I relish Sunday mornin' at home, with my old man messin' in an' out of the house. See you tomorrow—unless you changes your mind.

Mrs Bolders goes off to the bar

Leila goes slowly to the chair by the table and sits. She grips the arms as she tries to give herself strength

Trudi comes in from the bar

Trudi Mrs Bolders say she goes home.
Leila Yes. (*She gets up*) That's right, Trudi. I thought you and I could manage. Do you mind? It's a break for Mrs Bolders.
Trudi (*a little sullenly*) I don't mind. It does not matter to me what I do.
Leila Good. We'll have a cup of coffee and then just do only what is necessary. The rest can be done tomorrow.
Trudi (*turning to the door*) Very well.

Leila turns quickly up to the window as she hears a car arriving

I think you would not be so pleased for me to work in the bar if Bridget had been here.
Leila Trudi—please. I don't want to talk about her. Answer the door, will you?

Trudi goes off through the bar

Leila turns back to the window

Minnie Akers comes in. She has her golf bag, which she takes over and puts down above the desk

Leila stares across questioningly

Well?
Akers Who's here besides the Swiss girl?
Leila No-one; I sent Mrs Bolders home.
Akers (*nodding*) I see.
Leila (*urgently*) You haven't told me. (*Akers makes no sign. She goes over to her*) You said you were going to that place.
Akers I've been there. Clancy is dead.

Leila stares at her and sways unsteadily. Akers grips her by the shoulders

Leila (*quietly*) Then there's only one thing left to be done.
Akers Come and sit down. (*She helps Leila to the chair below the desk*) This time you've got to have a drink.
Leila (*nodding slowly*) Thank you. And after that I shall telephone the police.

Akers goes to the cabinet and gets a bottle and glass

So that woman was speaking the truth. (*With momentary emotion*) And I was praying to God you were right in what you thought!

Akers makes no comment, but pours out a drink

She's there—in that well-shaft?
Akers (*shortly*) She's there. (*She gives Leila the glass*)
Leila Thank you. (*She drinks it off. Then she gets up and goes slowly towards the window. She looks out for a moment, then starts to laugh a little hysterically*) That woman's gone to bury her. And while she's gone, I'm getting together the five thousand pounds I haven't got!
Akers You don't have to tell me she's gone there. I passed her on the way back.
Leila I see. Thank you for all you've done, Miss Akers.

Leila moves towards the phone, but Akers stands in front of the desk

Akers I haven't finished yet.
Leila Don't try and stop me, please. I am going to phone the police.
Akers No! I'll tell you when to phone the police.
Leila You're not being very kind. There's not a lot more of this that I can stand.
Akers I'll stop you phoning the police even if I have to rip this cord out! Now sit down. Over there, away from the phone.

Leila moves away slowly, then turns

Leila It's hopeless. You want to help me—but it's hopeless.
Akers It's not! Go on, sit down.

Leila sits in the chair by the table

Act III

Trust me, for God's sake, trust me. (*Quietly*) When the time comes I'll phone. Don't you worry about that. In the meantime I want you to be very quiet and calm. You're going to get out of this, my girl. Understand? But you've got to trust me as you've never trusted anyone in your life.

The doorbell rings. Akers goes quickly to the window

It's not that woman and your car. Who is it? Is there anyone to answer it?

Leila Trudi.

Akers Damn. (*She comes away from the windows*)

Mrs Fountain comes in from the bar. She stands at the door and looks questioningly across at Akers

Fountain It would be better if you told me, wouldn't it, Miss Akers?

Akers Told you what?

Fountain Exactly what is going on. I'm not a fool, and I hope you're not one. But there is something extremely unusual going on and somebody owes an explanation.

Leila (*half rising*) Very well, Mrs Fountain . . .

Akers Sit down! You, too, if you feel like it. (*She goes to the desk and starts dialling at the phone*)

Fountain What are you supposed to be doing?

Akers You'll know soon enough if you listen. (*On the phone*) Dorchester Police Station? . . . This is Miss Akers, The Treasure Chest, Helford-Abbas. I wish to report finding a dead body.

Mrs Fountain gives a gasp

Where? Look, I'm in *The Hay Wain* in the village and I'll stay until you come. Oh, and I'm here with Mrs Fountain of Oxley Court, the J.P. (*She listens for a moment, then replaces the receiver*) Coming right away. (*Rising*) Thought I'd better put you in the picture.

Fountain What is this? A dead body?

Akers Very dead. Bridget Clancy, the woman who poured out our drinks on Friday night.

Fountain An accident?

Akers Maybe, maybe not.

Leila I can tell you all about it, Mrs Fountain . . .

Akers (*sharply*) You could, but you're not going to. So kindly leave it to me.

Fountain Just a moment. You're taking a lot on yourself.

Akers (*nodding*) You can say that again. A hell of a lot. Care to sit down, Mrs Fountain?

Fountain No.

Akers Suit yourself. Only have the goodness to hear me out. The police'll be here in—what?—(*looking at her watch*)—twenty minutes. (*She sits on the edge of the desk*) I want you to leave this to me, Mrs Markham.

I'm going to tell everything. That woman Cousins is a blackmailer. She found out some bogus story about Mrs Markham and has been trying to force money out of her ever since she came here on Friday night. I believe Clancy was in on it...
Fountain We're talking about a dead body.
Akers That's right—Clancy. Mrs Markham shot her in this room yesterday morning.
Fountain I don't believe it!
Akers (*with emphasis*) She did it because she was being attacked. With a broken bottle. Right, Mrs Markham?
Leila (*in a low voice*) Yes.
Akers (*getting off the desk and moving up*) Well, you see, Cousins jumped in on that piece of luck. It was the chance to tighten the grip. She carts Clancy off in the car with the idea of going to the nearest hospital. But as Clancy died *en route*, she dumps the body at the building site near here and comes back to up the price as a payment for silence.

There is a silence

Fountain This is a terrible story. Mrs Markham . . .? (*She is about to address Leila but turns sharply to Akers*) You had no right to keep this from me.
Akers (*shrugging*) You're a J.P., not a cop.
Fountain Nor, I am pretty sure, are you.
Akers No. But I've got as much sense as anyone in this village—more than most.
Fountain (*helplessly*) Well, we can only wait.
Akers That's right. (*She glances at her watch and goes up to the window. She is anxious about an arrival and it may not be the police*) Not too long, though. I'd like to talk to Trudi, Mrs Markham, if you don't mind.
Fountain The Swiss girl? What for?
Akers (*laconically*) Evidence.
Fountain (*going up to her*) Now, just a moment! I've borne with you so far, but this is too much. I expressly forbid you to interfere in judicial matters.
Akers Sorry, my dear. You can forbid all you like, but I'm going to do it. The police have been called and they're on their way. That lets you right out, so if you don't like what I'm doing—go home.
Fountain (*repressing an outburst*) I'll have something to say about this.
Akers I bet you will. (*She goes across to the bar door, opens it and calls*) Trudi!
Leila (*wearily*) Miss Akers, please, let's just wait here until the police come.
Akers Don't you want to save something out of this ghastly situation? Don't you? Perhaps save everything? But for God's sake let me try my way.

Trudi comes to the bar door

Act III

Mrs Fountain moves angrily away to above the cabinet, as though determined to isolate herself from such illegal proceedings

Come in, Trudi.

Trudi looks from one to the other

Go and sit over there for a moment. (*She points to the chair below the desk*) Don't be alarmed.

Trudi goes over and sits

I only want to ask you one or two questions.
Trudi It's about Bridget, isn't it?

Mrs Fountain turns sharply

Akers Now, what made you say that?
Trudi She has gone away—perhaps for ever.

Akers moves above the table to a position between it and the desk

Akers Trudi, did you know that Mrs Markham kept a revolver in this house?
Trudi I do not understand.
Akers *Geschutz?*
Trudi Yes.
Leila Of course she knew it! I told her.

Akers holds up her hand for silence

Trudi Mrs Markham say it was in case of *einbrecher*—thieves. I think everyone know about it.
Akers Ah. You wouldn't know where she keeps it, would you?
Trudi Pardon?
Akers Where—does—she—keep—it?

Trudi gets up and goes towards the desk

All right.

Trudi returns to her seat. Akers pulls open the desk drawer and takes out the revolver. She extracts a couple of shots and then returns them

I hope the police won't mind me doing this.
Fountain There are a good many other things the police won't like!
Akers (*ignoring it*) What time was the shooting yesterday, Mrs Markham?
Leila I don't know.
Akers (*sharply*) Yes, you do.
Leila About—oh, I don't know—about half-past ten. Does it matter?
Akers It's vital. Did Clancy come from the bar? (*She waits*) I asked you . . . ?
Leila Yes, yes! She had been working there.
Akers Trudi, were you in the house at ten-thirty in the morning?
Trudi I go out.
Akers Where?

Trudi (*flaring up*) Where? Where? I go out.
Akers (*gently*) I'm only asking because it's important. It's nothing against you.
Trudi I write a letter to my mother in Basle and Mrs Markham say I can post it. So I go.
Akers Only to the post office? Please.
Fountain (*breaking in*) This has gone quite far enough! What you're doing is completely illegal . . .
Akers (*losing her composure*) For God's sake! Look, the police are on their way. I'm interfering in a serious matter. All right! But I believe I know something vital. All I ask is to be left alone for five minutes.

There is a silence. Mrs Fountain glances at her watch and moves up to the window

Well, Trudi, was your walk just to post a letter?
Trudi No. I go to try and find Bridget.
Akers Bridget Clancy. And what was so important about that?

Trudi hesitates for a moment, then bursts out

Trudi She owed me money! Fifty pounds. I needed it bad for my mother!
Akers I see.
Trudi My mother is ill!

Akers lets Trudi calm a little before going on

Akers And did you find her?
Trudi No. They tell me at the pub she has not been there for two days.

Akers is trying to work out her next line of enquiry, and the pause gives Mrs Fountain an opportunity to intervene

Fountain It's fifteen minutes since you phoned Dorchester. (*Moving towards the bar door*) I'm going to get the local man . . .
Akers (*sharply*) No. This is too big for any local man.
Fountain But not too big for a meddling woman!

Akers gives her a sharp look. She then sits on the edge of the desk and looks at Trudi

Akers About that walk, Trudi. Not a very nice morning, was it? I mean, I'm pretty certain it was raining hard at that time.
Trudi Yes, it was raining.
Akers Then didn't you get very wet?
Trudi Wet? Not so much. I had a raincoat.

Mrs Fountain makes a sudden movement to the window as she hears a noise outside

Fountain It's that young woman.
Akers Now, listen, everybody. We have reached the crisis point. Rightly or wrongly, I beg you to leave this to me.

Act III

Fountain She'll have to be told. The police may regard her as a witness . . .
Akers (*quickly*) Then tell her.

Cousins comes in from the bar

No-one moves. Cousins jerks a little in surprise at finding so many there, but she conceals it

Cousins Well. Interrupting something, am I? Don't mind me. I've just come to collect my baggage from upstairs and then I'm off. (*She moves towards the door* L)
Fountain We don't know your name.
Cousins Mrs Markham does. I'm Ruth Cousins, and I stayed here the weekend.
Fountain Miss Cousins.

Cousins, her hand on the door handle, turns

You'll have to know, because the police are on their way. Mrs Clancy, the help in the bar here, has been killed.

Any slight reaction from Cousins is covered by Trudi, who gasps and rises from her chair. Akers puts her arm round her and forces her gently back

Trudi Bridget—dead?
Akers All right, my dear; you'll get your fifty pounds, even if I have to give it myself.
Cousins That Irishwoman in the bar? Well, how did it . . . ? Look, I had no more to do with her but just order drinks, but . . . Sure there's no mistake?
Akers Death doesn't make mistakes.
Cousins God. Well! (*She looks round at the others*)
Fountain I'm sorry you should be dragged into this, but I'm afraid you ought to stay. The police will want to question everyone in the house.
Cousins Oh, sure, sure. Coming, are they?
Fountain From Dorchester. They've been phoned.
Cousins Oh, boy, why did I have to get caught up in this? (*She sits on the* L *arm of the settee*) Oh, I'm sorry. Bit shocked, too. I mean . . . Well, what the hell was it—car?

Mrs Fountain is about to say what is known, but Akers forestalls her

Akers No; it wasn't a car.
Cousins (*shrugging*) Well, these things happen. Only thing is, I'd like 'em not to happen when I'm spending a quiet weekend in a pub.

As there is no comment, she looks round at the motionless group

You know, if it wasn't bloody serious it'd be funny. I hardly know you lot. Mrs Markham, yes; she's the landlady. And the foreign kid—I mean, what are we all sitting here for?
Fountain The police.
Cousins Ah—sure.

Fountain There's no need to keep Trudi here. As long as she doesn't leave the house . . .
Akers Wait a minute. Just one or two more questions.
Fountain Miss Akers, the police will do that . . .
Akers Of course. But I'm going to ask them all the same. Tell us about that letter to your mother, Trudi.
Trudi I write it and go to post it. In the evening.
Akers And did you—post it?

Trudi looks at her, bewildered

Come, you must know.
Trudi (*trying to think*) I—I go first to the pub. (*She looks up in some alarm*) I can't remember.
Akers Perhaps in your anxiety you forgot it? Perhaps it's still in your pocket.

Trudi feels instinctively in her pocket

No; wouldn't it be in your raincoat pocket?
Trudi Yes—yes, of course.
Akers Fetch it for us, will you, dear.

Trudi hesitates, then gets up and goes to the bar door

Fountain There's no point in this! And it's blatantly criminal!
Akers Go on, Trudi.

The door is left open as Trudi goes out. She returns almost at once

Trudi It is not there.
Akers Perhaps in your bedroom?
Trudi No. It was not my raincoat. I borrowed Mrs Clancy's coat from the passage.

Akers moves up above the desk. There is a look of complete triumph on her face

Akers All right! Thank you, Trudi; you may go. But don't leave the house.

Trudi goes off to the bar

(*With satisfaction*) What the police will call "a material witness'.
Cousins I may be a bit dim, but I don't get all this.
Leila Do you want me to speak, Miss Akers?
Akers All in good time.
Cousins Well. (*She gets up*) I'll leave my address, and the police can get in touch with me. If they want to. But I saw no accident anywhere round here, so I don't reckon they will.

Act III

Akers (*quietly*) Please stay, Miss Cousins.
Cousins Oh, come on! This is getting a drag.
Akers I'm sure Mrs Fountain will ask you to stay. She is a J.P.
Fountain (*perplexed*) Well—look, Miss Akers and I don't agree at all about this. In fact the whole business is most illegal; but I do think you should remain here until it has been properly investigated...
Cousins Look, missis, you may be a J.P. and all that, but you've got no right to direct me. Or to try and hold me here. I got things to do and I'm going. Accidents happen every day, and the only ones concerned are them as sees them.
Akers Say I were to tell you it wasn't an accident? It was murder.
Cousins Eh?
Leila (*desperately*) No! You can't say that...
Akers But I do say it. Anyway, let's just say there was a shooting. You'll say there was a shooting, won't you, Mrs Markham?
Leila Yes. In this room.
Cousins In this room? Clancy, or whatever you call her?

Leila hesitates. She recognizes, blindly, that she is in Akers's hands

Akers (*prompting*) Go on; tell us exactly what happened.
Leila (*commencing in a low voice, then going on strongly*) It was yesterday morning. She was in the bar and had been drinking. She forced her way in here. Demanded money—lots of money. She said that she knew things about me and that if I didn't pay her... Then she broke the end off a bottle and came to attack me... (*She breaks for a moment, then goes on*) I shot at her. I had to. She meant everything she said.

There is a pause

Akers And now you're going to tell us what happened after that, aren't you?
Leila That woman—(*jerking her head in Cousins's direction*)—came in. She said Clancy was badly hurt and that she would take her to a hospital in my car...
Cousins That's a bloody lie! (*She stares round at the others*) God! What is this? Is the woman round the bend?
Akers (*breaking in*) Did she take her to a hospital? Or did she say Clancy had died on the journey and so she had hidden the body somewhere not far from here?
Leila Yes.
Cousins No! (*She is shaken, but she loses nothing of her natural tenacity*) A right lousey frame-up! This bitch has a spot of trouble in the house and she sees a chance of bringing a stranger into it. Just because it was a stranger who happened to put up here for the night. Someone nobody knew! And a pack of old tabs has to listen to her. (*She has completely recovered her confidence*) Would you believe it? Me! Took a bit of trouble off her hands and went and buried it for her. How kind. (*Viciously*) Why the hell should I do that?

Akers Because you were blackmailing her about her past life and you saw the chance to make the price higher.

Cousins looks at her, sizing up this dowdy little woman who is obviously the one she has to deal with

Cousins Go on; tell me more. Was I the one who come in here and shot her?
Akers No.
Cousins Ta, very much. (*Looking round at the company*) Well, like I said, I'm going now. That woman can tell her fancy tale to the police, an' I wish 'em luck picking the bones out of it.
Fountain All the same, I must insist you stay...
Cousins No-one insists anything with me, missis, so get that straight. As for pussy here, I reckon she'd be better off in a looney-bin.
Fountain (*moving up to the window*) Where are the police!
Akers They'll come—in good time.
Fountain It's over twenty minutes since you phoned them!
Akers Ah—yes. (*She moves without hurry to a position above the desk*) So all we have to do is wait.
Cousins (*dangerously*) I'm doing no waiting. Seems you and that nut-case are in cahoots to tie me up in something I knows nothing about. Bit of village aggro, eh? But I knows nothing about it and I leaves you with it. (*She moves below the table on her way to the bar door*)
Akers Without even collecting your things from the bedroom upstairs?
Cousins (*stopping and regarding Akers*) Reckon they can wait for another time.
Akers I can stop you going, you know. (*Without taking her eye off the other, she pulls open the desk drawer and takes out the revolver*) How about this?
Cousins (*steadily*) How about it?
Akers (*levelling the revolver*) I'm not a bad shot, you know. I can do other things besides sell antiques. Like clay-pigeon shooting. If you weren't in such a hurry I could show you cups I've won.
Cousins You soppy old trout. (*With a slow grin*) You don't scare me.
Akers No? (*Urgently*) Get up there by the window, Mrs Markham. Quick!

Leila joins Mrs Fountain by the window

Fountain Put that down, Miss Akers. This has gone far enough.
Akers I know what I'm doing. And it must be pretty plain to you now that this young woman knows far more about the death of Clancy than she's going to tell us...
Fountain Leave it to the police!
Akers The police aren't coming—not yet.
Fountain (*staring*) But you phoned them...
Akers I didn't, you know. You thought I did, but when I dialled I kept my finger on the receiver.

Act III   49

Cousins (*quietly*) Well, well.
Akers Because there's a bit more they should know when they do come.
Cousins Is that so? Then I'm almost sorry I shan't be here to listen to it. (*She goes over to the bar door then turns*) There's a car outside and I've got the key. It might be a good idea to put a few miles between me and this crazy set-up.
Akers (*levelling the revolver*) Say I stop you?

Cousins has her hand on the door, but her natural truculence gets the better of her. She faces Akers

Cousins Try. Go on, just try, you pathetic old crab!
Akers I told you I'm a good shot. You should be scared.
Cousins (*with an ugly laugh*) Like hell I am.
Akers No, I suppose you wouldn't be, seeing what's inside this revolver. Four blanks. Two of them were fired at Clancy by Mrs Markham that morning you rushed her to hospital. (*She tosses the gun back into the drawer*)

Cousins stands staring at her, uncertain of her next move

Clancy told you all about the gun that was kept in the drawer. So you got her to change the bullets for blanks. And then you worked up a fake wounding to step up the blackmail game. With fake gore, eh?
Cousins (*starting to move towards Akers*) Shut your...!
Akers Oh, no. (*She quickly turns to the golf-bag and draws out a shotgun*) I've just picked this up from my house, because I thought it might be useful. And this, you might as well know, *is* loaded.

Cousins stands rooted

Sit down, Miss Cousins. Over there, by the table. Sit down!

Cousins backs to the chair and sits

That's right. There's not so much difference between you and a clay-pigeon target except that you're a damned sight easier to hit. (*She sits on the edge of the desk, the shotgun resting on her knee*) You two over there, work your way gently to the settee and sit.

Mrs Fountain and Leila obey

That's right; we might as well be comfy. You needn't say any more, Mrs Fountain, because I think I've got all this buttoned up.
Cousins You think! You're crazy. Go on, phone the police, 'cos it's you they'll be carting off. (*Turning to the others*) Are you going to let this psycho get away with this? You know like I do she's just dreamed it up.
Fountain (*urgently*) Miss Akers, what's all this about blanks in the revolver? It doesn't make sense.
Akers Oh, yes, it does. I've told you, Mrs Markham did no more than

fire two blank shots at Clancy, who then acted as though she'd been badly hurt.

Fountain (*getting up and moving quickly above Akers*) But in that—that bogus call to the police, you said Clancy was dead.

Akers She is now. She's lying in a shallow grave at that new building site off the Malling Road.

Fountain How do you know? How, in heaven's name, do you know!

Akers Because half an hour ago I saw her lying there. She was only lightly covered with leaves and twigs. But on my way back in the car I passed that woman—(*pointing with the gun at Cousins*)—on her way in Mrs Markham's car to bury her properly. And she is properly buried now, isn't she, Miss Cousins? It was very necessary, seeing that sometime last night you shot Clancy dead. (*Keeping the gun levelled, she moves L of the settee*) Nothing to say?

Cousins is finished, but her voice trembles with suppressed fury

Cousins You damned bitch! It was her, sitting there. And you can't prove a thing against me!

Akers Oh, but I can. You see, Clancy is lying there wearing a raincoat. Trudi borrowed that raincoat to go out and post a letter. She put the coat back on the hook, and later last night Clancy came back here and took her property away.

Cousins No!

Akers Yes! I happened to look in the pocket of that raincoat. Why, I don't know, but I was just hoping to find something, anything. And the fact that will put you in prison for life is that in a pocket of that coat is the letter Trudi forgot to post! All of which is nothing to do with Mrs Markham, who is supposed to have shot her yesterday morning. The letter is waiting there for the police to ask about. They'll certainly ask you other things. Such as—did Clancy come back here last night to see you? Did she demand a bigger share of the blackmail? And did you find the only way to silence her was to get her out of this house and finish her? I don't know all these things—but the police will. And now, Mrs Fountain, I think it's about time we phoned Dorchester.

Mrs Fountain moves to the desk. Akers sits on the arm of the settee and levels the gun at Cousins

I'd do it myself, only I've rather got my hands full.

Mrs Fountain starts to dial, as—

the CURTAIN *falls*

FURNITURE AND PROPERTY LIST

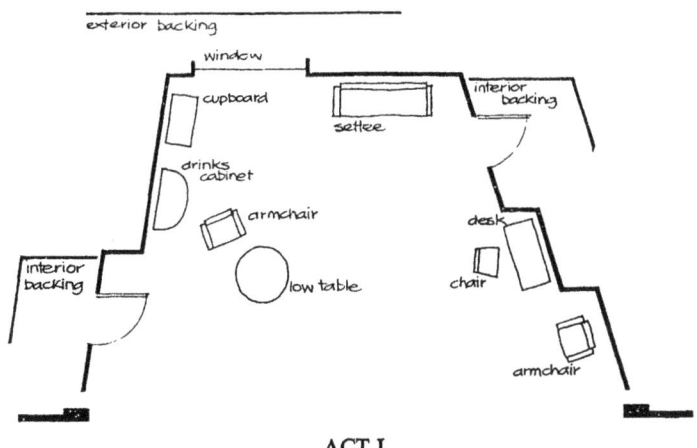

ACT I

Scene 1

On stage: Settee
Large armchair
Small armchair
Desk chair
Low table
Desk. *On it:* writing materials, papers, telephone, photograph of young girl in silver frame, small ornaments, cigarettes in box, lighter, ashtray, small antique silver salver. *In drawers:* loose cheque, cheque book, pistol, pound notes
Cupboard
Cabinet. *In it:* bottles of whisky, brandy, gin liqueur brandy, other drinks, soda syphon, tonic water, assorted glasses. *On top:* mirror
Carpet
Window curtains
On back wall: pictures, porcelain

Off stage: Carrier bag containing period pistol (**Akers**)

Scene 2

Strike: Dirty glasses

Set: Bottle of whisky and glasses on desk
Packet of £200 notes in desk drawer

Off stage: Tray of used breakfast things for one **(Trudi)**
Carrier bag with packet of £300 notes **(Akers)**

Personal: **Mrs Bolders:** handbag
Cousins: packet of cigarettes, lighter
Clancy: cigarette

ACT II

Strike: Dirty glasses

Set: Bottle back in cabinet

Off stage: Receipt **(Mrs Fountain)**
Car keys **(Cousins)**

ACT III

Strike: Receipt
Dirty glasses

Set: Bottles back in cabinet

Off stage: Tray of breakfast things for one **(Trudi)**
Bag of golf clubs with shotgun hidden inside **(Akers)**

Personal: **Akers:** magnifying glass, wristwatch
Mrs Fountain: wristwatch

LIGHTING PLOT

Property fittings required: wall brackets, desk lamp
Interior. A living-room. The same scene throughout

ACT I, SCENE 1. Evening

To open: General effect of early evening autumn light

Cue 1	After Curtain rises *Start slow fade to dusk throughout scene*	(Page 1)

ACT I, SCENE 2. Day

To open: General effect of autumn morning light

No cues

ACT II. Evening

To open: As opening of Act I, Scene 1

Cue 2	**Leila** turns on interior lighting *Slow fade to dusk outside window*	(Page 24)
Cue 3	**Leila**: ". . . money I haven't got!" *Bring up moonlight outside window*	(Page 32)

ACT III. Day

To open: As Act I, Scene 2

No cues

EFFECTS PLOT

ACT I

Scene 1

Cue 1	As Curtain rises *Noise of customers in bar. Repeat whenever bar door opens*	(Page 1)
Cue 2	After Curtain rises *Telephone rings*	(Page 1)

Scene 2

No cues

ACT II

Cue 3	As Curtain rises *Noise of customers as Cue 1*	(Page 19)
Cue 4	**Trudi:** "... never seemed the kind of person..." *Telephone rings*	(Page 20)
Cue 5	**Trudi:** "... *ich fur sie tun!*" *Doorbell rings*	(Page 20)
Cue 6	**Fountain:** "... done-up enough as it is." *Doorbell rings*	(Page 21)
Cue 7	**Leila** goes towards mirror *Telephone rings*	(Page 30)

ACT III

Cue 8	As Curtain rises *Sound of church bells. Fade shortly after action starts*	(Page 33)
Cue 9	**Trudi:** "I do the best I can..." *Doorbell rings*	(Page 33)
Cue 10	**Cousins:** "... I'll see you flattened." *Doorbell rings*	(Page 37)

Cue 11	**Leila:** ". . . if I shall ever see her again." *Car starts up and drives away*	(Page 38)
Cue 12	**Trudi:** "Very well." *Car draws up and stops*	(Page 39)
Cue 13	**Akers:** ". . . trusted anyone in your life." *Doorbell rings*	(Page 41)

www.ingramcontent.com/pod-product-compliance
Ingram Content Group UK Ltd.
Pitfield, Milton Keynes, MK11 3LW, UK
UKHW021848210426
5322IPUK00022B/528